THE HOLY TRAIL

THE CHALLENGE

the Holy Trail

12 LEGENDARY TRAILS
YOU SHOULD RUN

Rik Merchie

LANNOO

Table of contents

Italy & Switzerland
ULTRA TOUR
MONTE ROSA

170KM | 105MI • D+ 11,300M | 37,073FT
ULTRA & 4-STAGE RACE
100KM | 62MI • D+ 6,100M | 20,013FT

"While I was running
these trails around
Monte Rosa, my
training ground
for the UTMB®, I
thought this is the
race I would really
like to run. It didn't
exist so I've created
it for you to enjoy."

Lizzy Hawker

MY PUB

'If dogs run free,
then why not we?'

Bob Dylan

It's daybreak when my train worms out of the station of the Swiss town of St. Niklaus. I dive sleepy-eyed into the hood of my sweater. The past days have been a combination of kilometres, denivelations and hundreds of little orange flags. I'd not come to the Ultra Tour Monte Rosa (UTMR) to race, I'm not top runner enough for that, but rather to mark the route and help as a volunteer in an aid station. But with a mission: I wanted to listen to as many trailers as possible, to let drop the basic idea of my book and see if it took root in the international trail running community. And ask myself out loud what criteria I would use in selecting the trails for my book. Such editorial issues are better solved in the shadow of the Matterhorn than at a desk.

My publisher sent me off with the message that, for him, twelve races were more than enough. I nodded, but I had no idea of the standards that I would apply. Yes, to disregard the geographical boundaries of my home country - *ce plat pays* Flanders - seemed to me obvious even before I left. It's more fun to write about exotic trail races than about competitions in your own backyard.

Nor did I want to limit myself to existing competition series like the Migu Run Skyrunner World Series and the Ultra-Trail World Tour. And to discuss only the classic summer races in the Alps also seemed to me a too narrowly Western European framework. It was also clear to me that I wanted to cover as many distances and disciplines of trail running as possible - after all, ultra isn't the only thing that shines.

The blare of the train horn on entering a dark tunnel splits my head open. I blink and stare out crumpled. The reflection of my sunburned face in the window is interrupted only by the flickering fluorescent lamps hanging on the tunnel wall.

I'm thinking. In conversations with UTMR racers, I was challenged by the fact that in existing books about trail running it's often professional athletes who do all the talking. Inspiring, but I find stories of ordinary mortals more interesting. The stories of butchers, bakers and bankers who, in their spare time, retreat into nature to grind out running kilometres on unpaved paths. A human interest approach, with focus on the belly and tail of the race.

"Deal," my publisher said, "fits perfectly with the literary character of your personal texts for the book. And in this way the reader has some variety, with something else besides your own running adventures."

"OK, but I've written twenty texts. And you want twelve portraits of trail races in that book. How are we going to mix them? Do you want me to drop eight texts?"

"No, because I don't want to cut your story. We'll keep those twelve races and alternate with full-page photos of other races that are mentioned in the interviews or your texts. It's all about experience, isn't it?"

"That's pretty much it. OK, I'll buy it."

"And one more thing…"

"Yes?"

"You're writing not just for the world's diehards. Choose some competitions that normal mortals can handle after a year's training."

"Of course."

In my head I delete the words classification and ranking. The International Trail Running Association (ITRA) website lists hundreds of races. I've absolutely no intention of writing *The Holy Trail Bible* …

How in God's name do I decide which will be the first one? By distance or denivelation? With the organization and atmosphere as extra parameters?

No, I'd rather make an anthology of what is going on in this sport. What interests me is the poetry, not the rankings. More a pot pourri with different tastes and smells than a straight ranking.

Just like how a bartender tackles it.

A collection of 12 Grand Crus you can fall in love with. Without claiming there's no love outside the list, because every list is incomplete, and here and there with some extras as snacks.

Sorry, don't get you?

You expect a good bartender to have a number of classic cocktails on his menu. A margarita, a mojito and a Bloody Mary. You also hope he can recommend a tasty Saint-Emilion. A strong stout maybe? Or an exclusive whiskey from an obscure island with an unpronounceable name? Possibly a nip of the liqueur he homebrews from orange peelings? And concluding with an unknown artisan beer?

Welcome to *The Holy Trail*, my bar.

No compulsory purchasing from brewing multinationals. No promo deals. Just stuff that has attracted my attention in recent years, which I've gathered in my cellar as being good value and which I'd like to serve you.

RIK MERCHIE
SEPTEMBER 2017,
CHAMONIX-MONT BLANC, FR ▲▲▲

USA
HARDROCK HUNDRED MILE ENDURANCE RUN

161.7KM | 100MI • D+ 10,000M | 32,808FT

"You really have to embrace the unknown. You can try all you want to script it - how you see the day going and have these plans. But the mountains don't care. They're indifferent to whatever plans, whatever hopes you have..."

Timothy Olson

3, 2, 1...GO!

OR almost... 12 legendary trail races you should run?

For me there's no 'need to' about it, but yes, you've got up out of your armchair. Otherwise you would not have read this. Maybe you bought this book online or in a bookstore. Or you were given it as a present - maybe when you were sitting in your armchair, but the wrapping paper had to go into the waste bin. So yes, you had to get out of that armchair. * Well done!

* You regularly participate in trail races? Just finished a long distance run with hundred of metres of ascent and descent? Then stay the rest of the day in your armchair....

Now put on your running shoes and drag yourself outside. Again: well done! That was the hardest obstacle. You're halfway there already. Walk around a block. Stretch out on the way. Breathe deeply, in and out. Start jogging. The choice is yours: 5 minutes, 10 minutes... Then walk for a few minutes and repeat the previous step. And again. Return home after half an hour. Repeat the above the day after tomorrow. And again a few days later, but with up and down stairs. Or in a park with hills. A forest in a nature reserve? Even better! A mountain path? Absolutely! Congratulations, you're a trail runner... Now choose a race from the twelve legendary trail races in this book!

Excuse me?

Hold your horses!
Dreams are licit and necessary, but the races in this book are no walk in the park. All require solid training. Some trail races also demand specific technical knowledge and equipment. A well built-up running condition is an absolute pre-condition, even to consider taking part in these trail races. Without a good physical basis, you are likely to hurt yourself pretty fast. Or you will be disqualified from the race for being too slow. Or, from the first minutes you will be busy surviving rather than enjoying. Each of these scenarios has a great likelihood of legendary failure. And that's not what this book is about. But (re)start trail running. From 5 kilometres on to 10 kilometres. From 10 kilometres on to 20 kilometres. From 20 kilometres on to...*

* Are you having trouble counting in (kilo)metres? Have a look at page 209 for a conversion table.

Find the paths and play.
So you're already a road runner and are now moving to trail running?

Again, hold your horses!
You may already have sturdy running legs, but trails place different stresses on your body than asphalt does. On the road, your foot always lands in the same way, but not on an uneven trail. The constant search for balance on technical trails contorts your upper body into curves it's not accustomed to. In short: jump in, but for the first times, limit the number of kilometres to 50-75% of your usual distance.

Sign up for trail races that match your current physical condition. Who said that a 10 km race cannot be legendary? Check these calendars for a race in your neighbourhood:

WWW.BETRAIL.RUN
WWW.MUDSWEATTRAILS.NL
WWW.I-TRA.ORG

Afterwards, crawl back into your armchair with your acidic legs. Then take this book and fantasize which trail will disappear under your feet. Thousands of trail runners did so before you. Why couldn't you be one of them?

These ten pieces of advice should definitely help you on your way:

1. WALKING IS OK

Every trail runner is confronted with it sooner or later: a steep climb, where you simply have to walk. In fact, a practised trail runner will often prefer to walk rather than run uphill. This way he saves his strength, because usually there is more than one climb. Your heart rate and breathing, not the average speed on your sports watch, tell you whether your pace is right. Message to road runners: walking on trails is normal and nothing to be ashamed of.

2. KM, D+ & D-

The technical term in trail running is the letter D. This tells something about the level of difficulty of the race. In full, D stands for denivelation, which is the difference in height between two geographical points. This designation exists in two variants: a positive (D+) and a negative (D-). An example: A 30 km race with D+ 1,300 and D- 800 means that you will have to climb

"It's just running. You know how to run. No, really, you do. Left right."

Anton Krupicka

1,300 metres - in one or more separate climbs - over 30 kilometres and drop down - again in one or more descents - 800 metres. A useful tip for assessing a race: for every 100 D+ you can count a flat kilometre extra. Another example? If you were to take a rolling pin to the same 30 km race with 1300 D+ and roll it out flat, you would end up with the equivalent of a flat race of around 43 kilometres.

3. GEAR JUNKIES

Do you have to spend hundreds of euros in a sports store before getting started? No, because you can already go a long way with normal running shoes. However, if you want really to immerse yourself in this sport, some extra equipment is a good idea. It certainly pays to invest in a pair of trail running shoes. The deeper grooves offer more grip on slippery surfaces. In comparison with traditional running shoes they often have a lower drop. In this way you stand a little lower on the ground, which reduces the risk of a twisted ankle. It's also important that your running shoes fit tightly around your heel and that your toes at the front have enough room to expand during running. Ideally, your trail running shoes have a protective edge that prevents your toes from bruising after a few kilometres. An extra boon is a *rock plate*. This is a plastic fabric that ensures that sharp rocks and tree roots do not pierce the rubber of the outsole into your foot. Whether you opt for a lot of or little cushioning depends on your running style, body weight, terrain and the duration of your training or competition. Of course it's nice to have shoes that are as light as possible, but lightweight is not always long-lasting. Waterproof shoes with, for example, a Gore-Tex membrane look interesting at first sight, but if water runs into them from the top, it will stay. To cut a long story short: give serious thought to your trail running footwear, and be sure to visit a specialized dealer. Try different models, ask for advice and read reviews on the internet. *Barefoot* and *minimal trail running shoes*? Fun toys, but in the initial phase building up sensibly and alternating with your classic trail running shoes is the message.

The longer and the higher you go, the more equipment there is to recommend. Running backpacks and race vests with water bags, drinking bottles and other small bottles. Energy gels, powders and muesli bars. A running watch that indicates your route on GPS. Telescopic or folding running sticks to hoist yourself over that mountain crest. A lightweight jacket against wind squalls along the way, sunscreen and sunglasses with a high UV index, and a headlamp compared with which car headlights are fairy lights. A survival blanket and whistle for emergency situations. A trail running shop is a paradise for *gear junkies*, but not for your credit card. Thinking carefully about what you do and do not buy is healthy, saving on safety in inhospitable terrain is not.

4. BEER AND SAUSAGES

A trail race is not about dieting. Sumo wrestling aside, there is no other sport where you have to eat and drink as much. In road races, the offerings in the aid stations are often limited, but with (longer) trail races, aid stations are often bacchanals. Tea, broth, cola, sports drink and water. Slices of cake, sausage and cheese, orange segments, nuts, crisps and dry salt biscuits. On extremely long runs soup and pasta also at times. Eat and drink well also outside the aid stations.

Practice this during your training sessions, because during your race you don't want to be learning what works and what doesn't work for your stomach. Beer and sausages are best kept for after the race. Or avoided totally.

5. WHAT GOES UP, MUST GO DOWN

If the path is not too steep, dribble with short, quick steps uphill. Should you switch to walking? *Fair enough:* Hands on the thighs and push! On simple descents you can use wider steps. Use gravity and let the slope do the work. Don't forget to breathe, because some runners have the reflex of holding their breath on descents. On technical and steep descents it's advisable to take shorter steps and stretch your torso as long as possible, as if running down a staircase. Try to move lightly. That way you are quick, but also agile so as to respond accurately to swishing branches and loose pebbles. It can be very tempting (and fun) to turn onto *full power* downhill, but you can also trip quickly - especially as a beginner. So let your speed grow with your experience.

6. SCAN THE PATH AHEAD

A motorcyclist doesn't stare at his front wheel, but looks far ahead to be able to anticipate what will happen. In the same way, trail runners are best advised not to look at their feet while running. Always look four or five steps ahead so that you know what's coming at you. Take care not to bend too much, because then not enough air gets to your lungs.

7. CORE STABILITY

To be able to respond quickly and agilely with your feet, you need a strong core. Logical, because all those G-forces on that winding and unstable path don't stop at your navel. A solid house has a foundation of steel and concrete. Invest in *core stability*. Planking, and more planking. Simple.

8. FEET & ARMS

Tripping and falling is part of trail running, but raise your feet sufficiently while running and you've come a long way. Your arms help give you balance. Good use of the arms is therefore extra important in trail running. On technical terrain you will find more balance by holding your elbows wider apart. On descents, keep your arms level with your chest with your hands slightly outwards. On slopes with lots of obstacles, lower your arms a little.

9. TRAIN YOUR SKILLS

Just as interval training boosts your speed for road races, repetitions on a technically challenging trail boost your technique. Focus on your posture and, like in skiing, find the right line and flow for you. Complete your running training with strength and balance exercises.

10. CHILLAX

Altitude and distance are your enemy, not your fellow runners. Trail races can be just as competitive as road races, but the atmosphere is more friendly and relaxed. And we'd like to keep it that way. Learn to share the path with other users, help colleagues in need, keep your waste with you and thank the volunteers. ▲▲▲

Italy

TOR DES GÉANTS®

356.3km | 221.5mi • D+ 27,390m | 89,862ft

"Tor des Géants® is made of pain and smiles, hugs and glances. It is made of faces and landscapes encountered along one's own path. It is a challenge to your emotions, it is the deep desire to leave without being sure to arrive."

TOR DES GÉANTS 2017
OFFICIAL VIDEO REPORT

BACKPACK

My train's leaving in an hour's time. I've been packing for three days now, but my apartment floor still looks like an outdoor sports store in which a bomb has exploded.

Come on, get on with it.

Basics first: tent-sleeping bag-roll mat. No attempt on the summit without a base camp. Gas stove, cooking set and pasta. Lots of pasta. Plus sugar waffles, granola bars, crisps and dates.

Running backpack with drinking bottles and water bladder with drinking tube. I tot it up in my head. One litre at the front and two litres at the back as maximum capacity for complete autonomy. Three litres is already three kilos extra weight. I'm no gram chaser, but man does not live on water alone. Four apple-flavoured energy gels with calcium and magnesium, five cola-flavoured energy gels with caffeine, three chocolate-flavoured power bars and a packet of salty cookies to get through the day. Pills with a concentrate of essential amino acids. Effervescent tablets to replenish the electrolytes. Valerian capsules for a good night's sleep. An equal number of Traumeel® anti-inflammatory tablets. And, for the finale, an extremely strong coffee-tasting energy gel with a triple dose of caffeine. Not to forget: sports tape, tiger balm, massage cream, factor 50 sunscreen and lip balm.

A bottle of red wine for the soul and a jar of anti-friction cream for the scrotum.

I feel like I've just raided a pharmacy. I stuff everything in my trekking backpack. Meanwhile, a Rock Werchter version of *Feel Good Hit of the Summer* by *Queens of the Stone Age* thunders at volume 11 through my kitchen.

You need some porno music…
Everybody knows you dance like you fuck,
you dance like you fuck, you dance like you fuck…

O, yeah…

So, how do you fuck in Belgium?
That's what I wanna know!

O, come on, you must fuck better than that! How do you fuck in Belgium?
It's fucking good, that's what I know

Nicotine, valium, vicodin, marijuana, ecstasy and alcohol… Co-co-co-co-co-cocaine

Choice of tyres?

My minimal 4 millimetre drop lightweight competition shoes or my robust 10 millimetre drop training shoes? The first pair are better for clawing uphill, the second more comfortable in long descents. And what about my normal running shoes? Not that I expect lots of asphalt, but still. Useful for limbering up the day before the race.

Eventually I stuff three pairs of running shoes into my backpack.

• Short and long running pants.
• Rain jacket with hood.
• Two quick-drying T-shirts.
• Two pairs of running socks.
• Cap and gloves.
• MP3 player with earphones.
• Telescopic running poles.
• Headlamp.
• Sunglasses.
• Bandana.
• Folding drinking cup.

Check.

Medical certificate in English, whistle for distress signals and aluminium survival blanket.

Double check.

I'm travelling and take it all with me.

And, last but not least, because it was just my luck that my number came up in the lottery: a starting ticket for an exclusive ultra-marathon in the mountains. ▲▲▲

"I'm no gram chaser, but man does not live on water alone."

Norway
TROMSØ
SKYRACE

Badass bromance between sea and sky

Tromsø
TROMSDALSTIND SKYRACE

28km | 17.4mi • D+ 2,000m | 6,561ft

- Trail legends Kilian Jornet and Emelie Forsberg as race directors
- Small-scale and charming
- Alpine terrain, but too low to give you altitude sickness

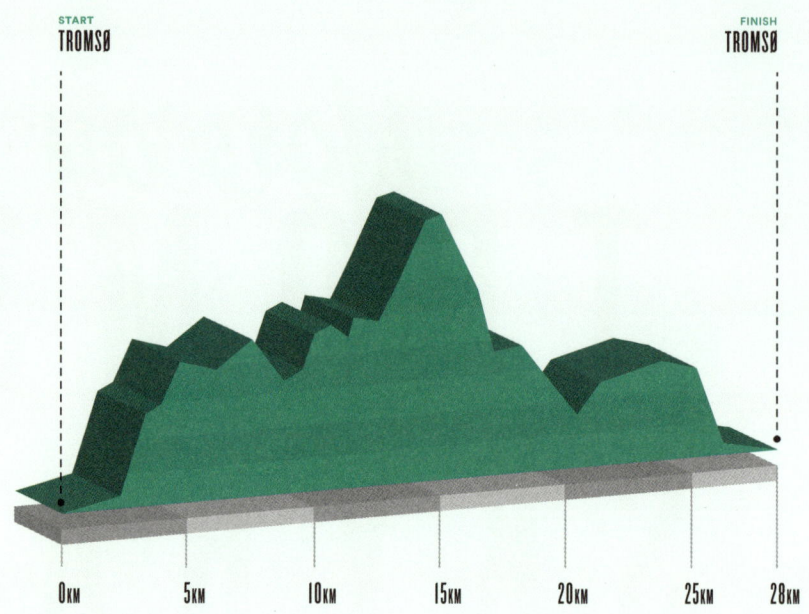

START
TROMSØ

FINISH
TROMSØ

0km   5km   10km   15km   20km   25km   28km

OTHER DISTANCES

HAMPEROKKEN SKYRACE
57km | 35.4mi • D+ 4,800m | 15,748ft

BLAMANN VERTICAL
2.7km | 1.7mi • D+ 1,044m | 3,425ft

BØNTUVA SKYRACE
15km | 9.3mi • D+ 800m | 2,624ft

BRIAN LANG
Age 28 • Doctoral student
Baldwinsville, New York • USA

Why did you choose this race?

BRIAN "Gosh, long story... I've been living in Basel in Switzerland for a few years now for my doctoral research. Earlier as a student I used to do athletics. Besides track I'd also run some modest half-marathons, so running was already in my legs. Together with an American friend, I wanted an excuse to explore Switzerland. I saw pictures of the Sierre-Zinal trail race online and we were immediately sold. In the same year, 2015, we also ran the Jungfrau Marathon. Then I started sniffing around on the internet to see what trails there are outside Switzerland.

I've always been fascinated by these high fjords in Scandinavia and that's how I came across Tromsø. A skyrace, from sea level up the cliffs. I was immediately sold! As I clicked further, I saw the competition had four events. A vertical kilometre and a 15 km race seemed a bit trivial to justify the long journey. The very technical Hamperokken Skyrace with 57 km and 4,800 metres vertical climb is the crown jewel, but I didn't see myself as up to it. This left the Tromsdalstind Skyrace. One peak instead of two and only - yes, 'only' - 28 km and 2000 metres vertical climb. We registered the same day for the 2016 race (laughs)."

How did you prepare?

BRIAN "I may have done Sierre-Zinal and the Jungfrau Marathon, but the Tromsø Skyrace is a different kettle of fish. In places it's more scrambling than running. If I wanted to pull it off, I'd have to train seriously. With eight months to go, I started training in December. Too ambitiously, it turns out, because after two weeks I started secretly skipping training sessions until I finally did nothing more. In February I got a grip on myself again and achieved weeks with over 50 km. In March and April it fell back to 30 km a week until in May we were back to where we started. June was a wake-up call in which I consciously did a lot of vertical climb. The last month before the race I was back with my family and friends in the US. With the many visits and parties I never once pulled on my running shoes. I assumed it would all work out. The cut-off time was 12 hours. But surely you can walk 28 km in 12 hours? With my substandard training it would not be a fast race, but rather a test of my endurance and grit."

How did your race go?

BRIAN "Actually you run from sea level to the top of the Tromsdalstind. That's a solid 1200 metres climb. With my poor preparation in the back of my mind, I restrained myself, but after the summit came a long technical descent in which I wanted to assert myself and live it up. I'd

Race secret

The water in the rivers on the trail is so pure you can drink it straight out. Ideal for rinsing the different wild berries* you'll find along the course.

*Unless Emelie Forsberg has picked them all for her cakes.

never seen anything like this before: a big wasteland of boulders, sometimes with a half metre height difference from one step to another. After this there were just 10 kilometres to go. What did I have to lose? Back down at the bottom, I could hardly take another step. My thighs were exploding. Running was impossible. Jogging was still just about doable..."

Which moments will you never forget?

BRIAN "Most competitions serve dried fruit, candies, chocolate and muesli bars in aid stations. All sweet things, while I prefer salty flavours. That's why I had a bag of sun-dried tomatoes in my race pack. I still see myself wolfing them down in that misty landscape, I was so burned out. I ate almost all my supply at once. Maybe a bit weird to bring sun-dried tomatoes. Because they don't give a lot of energy, but it was the best snack of my life."

A golden tip for future participants?

BRIAN "For the last kilometres I again wanted to run a bit faster, to stay ahead of my standard.

Maybe after all those sun-dried tomatoes gave me the energy I needed? I barged through the nth river and jumped up the bank, where a mud zone followed. The foot with which I landed immediately sank in deep. Before I knew it I was into slush to above my knee. I lost my balance and fell forwards. It took a while before I realized what had happened. A frozen break-dance débutant in a muddy pose, that's what it must have looked like. Too bad there was no photographer in the area (laughs). So be extra careful when you see mud!"

"It was crazy, but it was awesome! Certainly one of the most difficult races in the world!"

Greg Vollet
SALOMON TEAM MANAGER

FOOTBALL

Cleaning up is not my favourite pastime. Reluctantly I force myself to undertake this seasonal task. On today's programme: the bookcase. Take back borrowed books, trace lost items and store new acquisitions.

And dust them all, as well.

As I work, I notice how my bookcase is bulging with running books. Roughly they fall into two categories: running books written by/about top athletes and running books with training and/or nutrition schedules.

The first category often feels out-of-this-world and slightly autistic. I'm anything but a super talent, whose sole kicks come from kilometres run and still to run. The second category is too perfectionist for me. I enjoy life too much to stick to their schedules. I'm a Burgundian at heart. I can be terribly nonchalant, but can also sink my teeth into a project like a bloodthirsty pit bull if I really want to. That's the straddle. I myself don't understand this symbiosis properly, but that's how it goes for me.

Running has been a lifebuoy a few times in my life, but I'm not the runner I find in my books. Surely there must be other people like me? Perhaps the French inventor of the trucker hats with the inscription *Run, Beer, Burger* is still the closest. Unfortunately his slogan lacks sufficient letters to be placed on the market as a book.

I wring out my cleaning rag. The water in my bucket is turning grey.

Three thick files lie on the bottom bookshelf. Now what was it they contained?

I roll the elastic band from one of the covers and open the file. Memorabilia of every kind from my primary school days tumble out. On the top is the home-made school newspaper that my classmates and I sold for five francs on the playground. I leaf through the A4 pages with their childish handwriting, smile and return in time to my first year in primary school.

We run every day!
We belong to a running club.
We run all the time in the playground and at home!

The runners' bosses

Pieter the number one boss
Rik the number two boss
Jeremie the general

Seven years old, just learning to write and immediately a big mouth. Even so I know my place in the hierarchy of our self-invented running club. Below Pieter, that's clear. He does athletics and is devilishly fast. I refer to Jeremie as a general. Not as boss, because he's not a classmate and not such a super strong runner either.

Jeremie and I are both swaying lights on the playground. Having been born premature, motor skills and co-ordination are not my strongest points. For that reason I often let football and volleyball pass me by. If as a child you're laughed at for catching or kicking air most of the time, you quickly crawl into a corner. Jeremie can handle a ball, but is often too brutal during the game. I took the battering ram under my wings many times when things worked out wrongly. In exchange, I had his strong fists to defend me in the jungle called primary school.

'YES? GO!'

Run. Just like playing football, but without a ball. Around the playground, between the cast iron poles of the awning. Roaring over the concrete tiles, bouncing across the lawn near the grotto of the Blessed Virgin Mary. Cutting each other off, accelerating, getting out of breath. And after a few rounds, crouching to re-tighten the velcros of your shoes. Slaloming between coquettish girls. Across hopscotch games, alongside milk-drinking toddlers.

Twenty years later I would read *Born to Run* - by far the favourite running book in my collection. In it American journalist Christopher McDougall takes the anthropological approach, discussing at length the weal and woes of the running Tarahumara Indians, who live in a corner of Mexico full of cobweb-like rock labyrinths. A conscious choice, please note. With the arrival of the Spanish conquistadores, the indigenous peoples had two possibilities: to fight or to flee. Unlike the Aztecs and the Mayas, the Tarahumara decided to run. Into the Copper Canyons, where they still live four hundred years on. Far away from all western influences, except for an occasional cocaine farmer and errant *Einzelgänger*.

Their ritual running competitions between villages, with cattle and corn as prizes, continued all these years. In their language: *rarajipari*. Not solo against the clock, but in teams of four or more, with a small leather ball pushed forward by the runners. Drinking like fish at night at a local fun fair and then a group run of at least 50 kilometres with a ball as a handicap.

Forget about football.
Bury rugby.
Bye bye marathon.

Men with balls do *rarajipari*.

'OUT OF THE WAY! CAREFUL!'

Pieter is the first to finish after a competition run. I'm second and entitled to his smug grin. Followed by a handful of playground colleagues who jumped onto our bandwagon on the way. And last home, a puffing battering ram: Jeremie.

The game is then repeated in less delicate format during PE lessons. On wafer-thin white gym shoes, which parents are required to purchase at the start of the school year for their offspring. Cheap *Made in Chinas*, because the family budget has no room for fast-growing children's feet.

"Today we are doing the Cooper test."

The playground is lined with orange cones. More than half of the class groans. Next to me, Joke pushes her glasses a bit higher.

"Who can tell me what a Cooper test is? Who remembers it from last year?"

A large number of football fingers go up.

"Yes, Joris..."

"Running as long as possible, sir."

"Almost... not as long as possible, but as far as possible in 12 minutes."

Tom raises his finger from the belly of the class: "For points?"

"Yes, it's a test for the report!"

Now everyone groans. Except for Pieter, who positions himself like a rooster on the starting line. Joris pulls up his yellow local football team socks. I position myself behind him. Maybe I should give football another try? I once got that far, but it went wrong. Plucking up all my courage, on a blue Wednesday afternoon, I stepped into the locker room of the local ball cuddlers, flanked by the duty child attendant. Only to learn that the training session was long past. For me confirmation that this sport wasn't for me. After that I never had the courage to try again.

'3, 2, 1, GO!'

Pieter rushes away. I wriggle my way between footballer legs. A ninety degree corner around the first cone. The front ranks brake and then speed up again. I feel Joke crash onto my shoulder with her glasses. Back into second and then third gear. If possible, fourth. The class spreads out like a ribbon as we pass by the remaining cones. After one more round, Pieter laps the chubbiest girl in the class.

"Another 9 minutes", our gym teacher roars.

I hang in the middle of the pack. Will I do well enough for a 3/10? I begin to count. Almost three rounds behind me. In 3 minutes. So 9 minutes left. The numbers slow me down. I feel caged and am afraid to fail.

Here I'm not second boss, nor a general. Here an emperor in real sports shoes holds sway. With a bunch of football players as body-guards. OK, in our club we sometimes make a competition of it, but only by accident. And never for points. This is not a game, but simply a way of giving marks to people. No adventure, but a bunch of hamsters in a treadmill. I'm blocked with my thinking.

"Another 4 minutes," sounds from the other side of the playground.

I catch up Jeremie. He's having a hard time of it. In my wake comes Jonas, with whom I write the school paper. Not an official member of our club, but in the running as a prospective member. Our faces are blood red. My throat feels like a grater.

"1 minute left!"

I squeeze myself round the cone. Come on! With the finish in sight, the desire for self-sabotage has subsided. One last effort, come on, Rik.

A few metres ahead of me Joke with her glasses is doing her absolute best. With a few seconds on the counter, it all goes wrong. In her absolute determination she misses her last cone. She splays out over the tiles. Tears and knees full of playground grit.

A curse on every form of education!

What's the betting that we'll simply play football during the next gym lesson?

Or will it be time for a game of *rarajipari*?

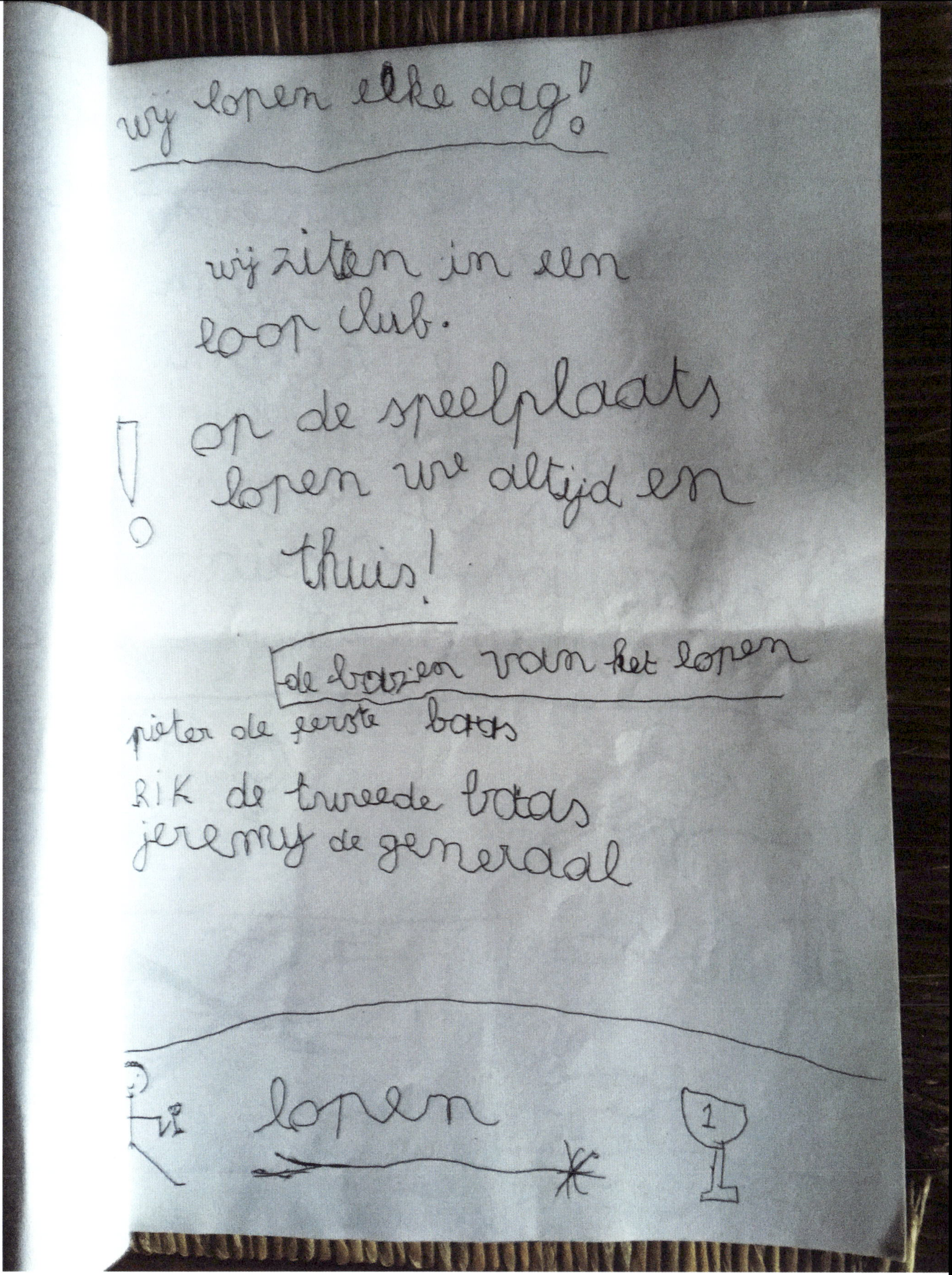

wij lopen elke dag!

wij ziten in een
loop club.

op de speelplaats
lopen we altijd en
thuis!

de bazen van het lopen

pieter de eerste baas

RIK de tweede baas
jeremy de generaal

lopen

1

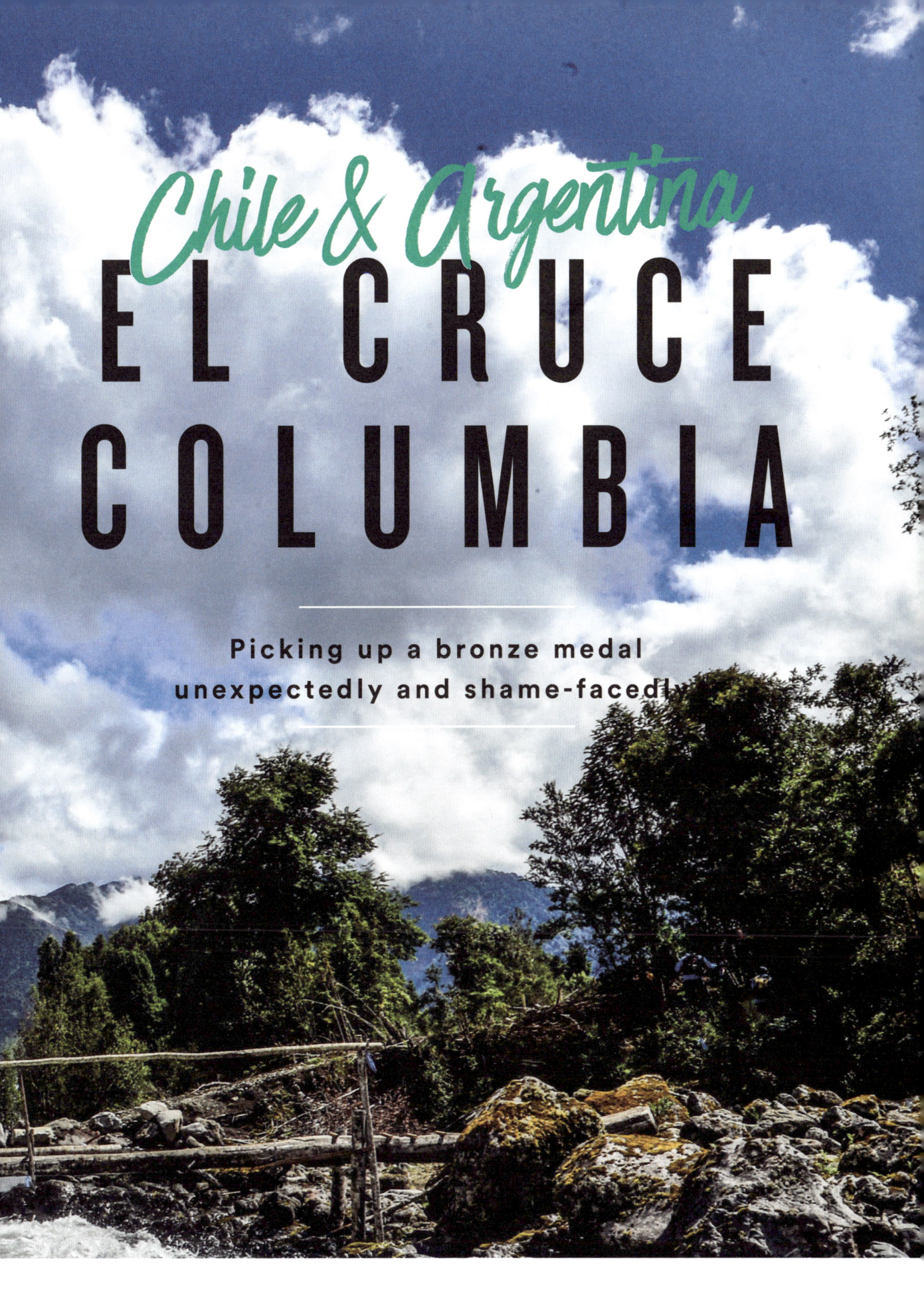

Chile & Argentina
EL CRUCE
COLUMBIA

Picking up a bronze medal
unexpectedly and shame-faced

Cerro Catedral
EL CRUCE COLUMBIA

104KM | 64.6MI • 3 STAGES
D+ 3,500M | 11,483FT

✚ Feasible multi-day race for beginners

✚ Very friendly tent camp

✚ Pat-a-go-ny!

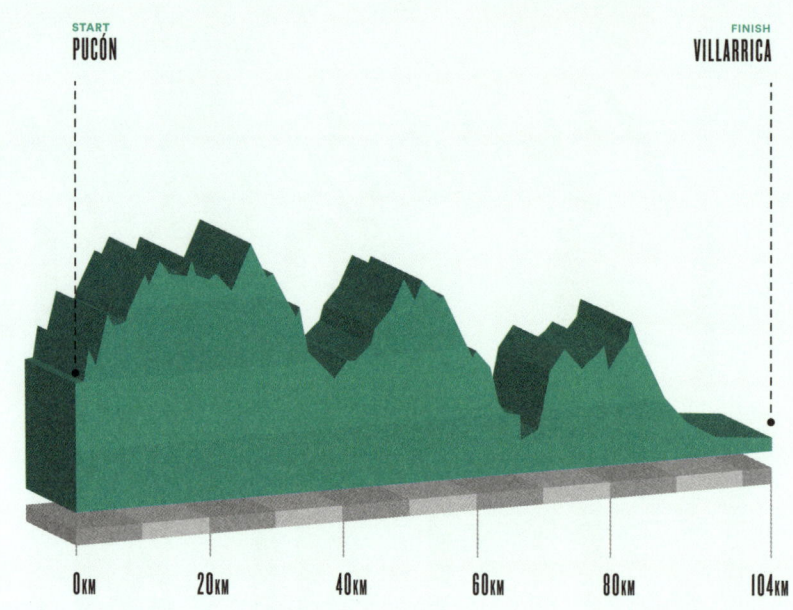

START
PUCÓN

FINISH
VILLARRICA

0KM   20KM   40KM   60KM   80KM   104KM

ROUTE EDITION 2018

DARIANNE SPITTAELS

Age 30 • Nurse
Ghent • Belgium

LOTTE SPITTAELS

Age 32 • Nurse
Ghent • Belgium

Why did you choose this race?

DARIANNE "How did it all start? We picked up the love of running from when we were kids. As a child, I ran along with my older sister Lotte when our dad started grinding rounds on the track. When we were older, we took the risk of joining runs and the like. From time to time, my sister did a trail race in the Belgian Ardennes, but never more than 15 kilometres. Not me, because by then I was playing high-level rugby and that's where my time went. Only when I stopped and went looking for a new challenge did I choose to run a marathon. My godfather came to watch. After I'd completed it, he told me of a friend of his who had once run a stage race somewhere in South America. That clearly stuck, because a few weeks later I called my godfather and asked him to put me in touch with his friend. That's how I learned that this competition takes place in the border region between Chile and Argentina and that El Cruce means 'the crossing' in Spanish. I looked it up online. That year's edition had just been run, so I had a full year to move up from 42 kilometres to 100 kilometres in three stages. I didn't see myself doing it all on my own. On their website, I saw there was a separate ranking for teams. I immediately called my sister. I knew that she would jump on the idea, and I didn't want to do it with anyone but her. For a race like this, it's important that you're on the same wavelength and can sense each other well. Who's better company than your own sister?"

LOTTE "In the end, we hesitated a long time before signing up. Only after your second marathon did you have enough self-confidence, right? Only then did I tell you with a cute note that I wanted to go for it too."

How did you prepare?

LOTTE "I'm not a person who plans things well in advance, but for this sort of adventure you have to. My sister had a sports doctor draw up a schedule for her. I more or less followed it with her. Four running sessions and one power training session a week, over a six-month period. My sister kept strictly to the preparation plan. She even went to fitness sessions. I alternated much more with yoga and cycling. Mostly we trained alone, but in the summer we went trekking together in the Alps. Long trips, day after day, with backpacks. It seemed like a good way to test just how well prepared we already were."

DARIANNE "The real test was a trail running training weekend in Spa. Three days in a row on the trails, with a program of 75 kilometres and 3,000 metres vertical climb. My sister had never run more than 22 kilometres, making that many back-to-back training sessions a real challenge."

LOTTE "For me it was extra exciting because I have an intolerance for refined sugars and cow's milk, which means that energy gels and power bars are out for me. I therefore had to make do with nuts and raisins, and honey diluted with water. Works best, though!"

DARIANNE "That training weekend scared us a bit. We were absolutely green behind the ears. Hearing one hair-raising story after another about famous ultras doesn't exactly boost your self-confidence. Fortunately, we passed quite a few of those experienced bigmouths on the final run. That gave us a boost (laughs). But not for long, because a month and a half before the race, I got problems with my knee. The cartilage in my knee joint looked to be damaged. The doctor advised against starting..."

LOTTE "Come on, sister! He didn't advise against, he forbade it!"

DARIANNE "Yes, whatever. But I wasn't ready to listen. I just had to run El Cruce. In the end, that doctor went along with my story. I then used all the forces in the universe to start. Physiotherapist, osteopath and personal coach. Support bandages and the largest possible dose of anti-inflammatory drugs. I tried to train, but often had to stop after just a few kilometres. As an ex-rugby player, I'm used to quite a lot, but the pain was too intense. During the last two weeks before the run, I didn't touch my running shoes. Mentally that was terrible, because you work so hard for something and then your body gives up."

Race secret

El Cruce has no fixed course. Many return to experience this race again. The cheapest way is to finish first in your category. Then the organization will offer to pay for your ticket for the next El Cruce.

LOTTE "Fortunately, we were not heading to South America just for El Cruce. Together with my sister's boyfriend, we were going to travel round for a month afterwards. We then agreed that we would start. If running proved too painful, we would simply walk. Walking a sharp 30 kilometres, three days in a row, without a heavy backpack; surely my sister could handle that."

How did your race go?

DARIANNE "The first day, the stage was split into two parts. One where you start in Chile and cross the border into Argentina. There, minibuses were waiting to ferry us to the second start, beyond the no man's land. between the borders. The running itself went well. Miraculously, I had no problem with my knee. What we did have to adapt to was the heat. Fortunately, the last kilometre ran through a river that ended up in a lake. After finishing, we simply floated in it to cool off."

LOTTE "After the first stage, we were eighth in the women's teams. We had to laugh about that anyway. What were we doing there, we little Belgians? We also felt anxious, because the other runners looked so professional. It only got worse, because after the second stage we had the second place in our category. My sister's knee just held out. Even with a climb of more than 1,000 vertical metres!"

DARIANNE "We were just three seconds ahead of the team in third place. For the last stage, we did everything we could to get silver, but finally it was bronze."

Which moment will you never forget?

LOTTE "After each stage, you're pampered enormously by the organization. Your tent is standing, your luggage is ready... There are a lot of employees to assist you with advice and practical help. Every night, there was an Argentinian barbecue or a party. All tightly organized! I still remember the opening ceremony. Every country had to provide a delegation to carry the national flag. We were the only Belgians, so there wasn't much discussion as to which delegation would do it. It was just like we were at the Olympics."

A golden tip for future participants?

DARIANNE "When registering, we had to give a name for our team. At first, we thought about *Dos Hermanas*, because we are two sisters. But in the end, we found that too predictable. We then chose *Los quesos duros*, Spanish for *The hard cheeses*. When we're in the mountains, we both like to eat these strong cheeses, that's why. It seemed funny to us to use an absurd name. Little did we know that *queso duro* is street language for dry sperm, or smegma, or something like that. We got many strange looks. Especially from the organizers when they called us onto the podium to receive our bronze medal (laughs). So be careful when you choose a name for your team!"

"A barbecue pit is set up to grill enough beef, chicken and chorizo to feed 1500 hungry runners twice a day. [...] It's the only race I've done where a 'cuchillo para carne' (steak knife) was on the packing list."

Amy Proston
SILVER MEDAL EL CRUCE 2014

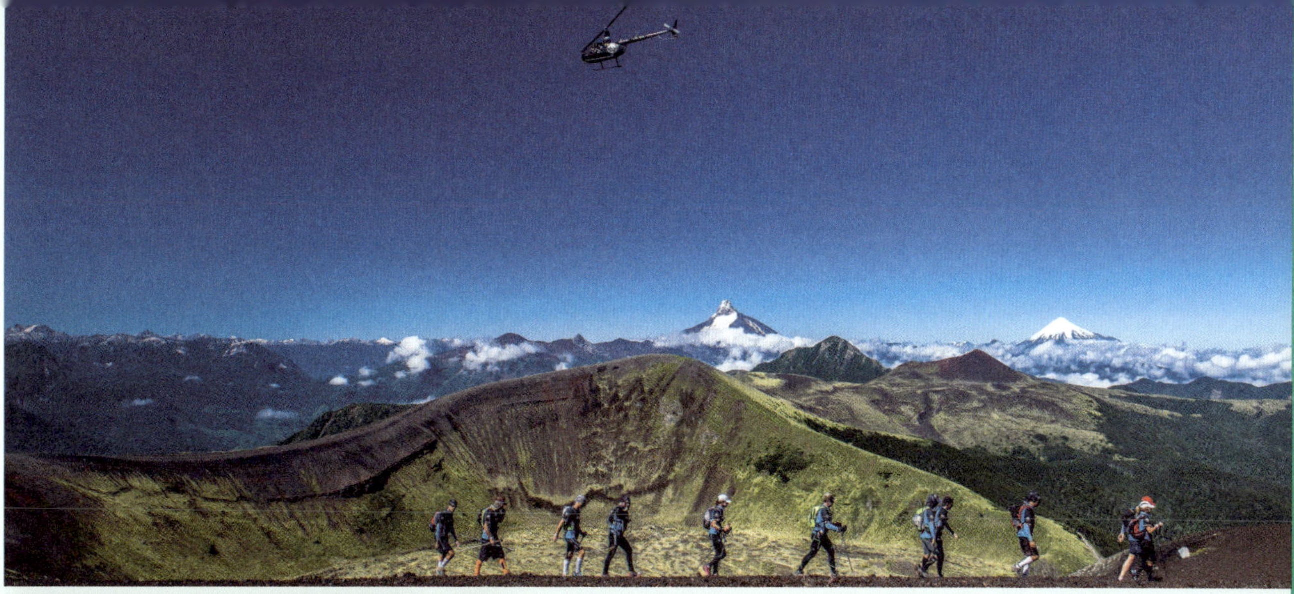

ARGENTINA
BIENVENIDO
A
CHILE

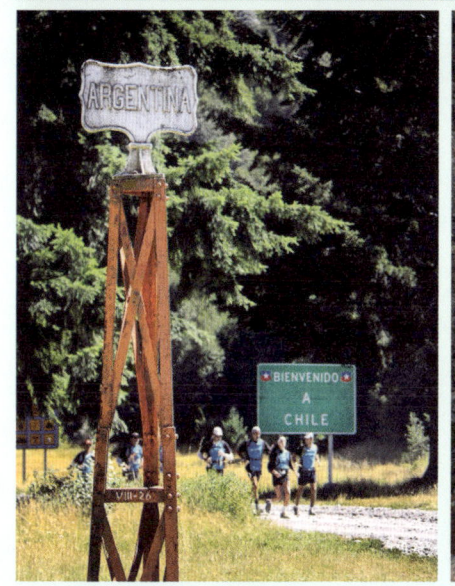

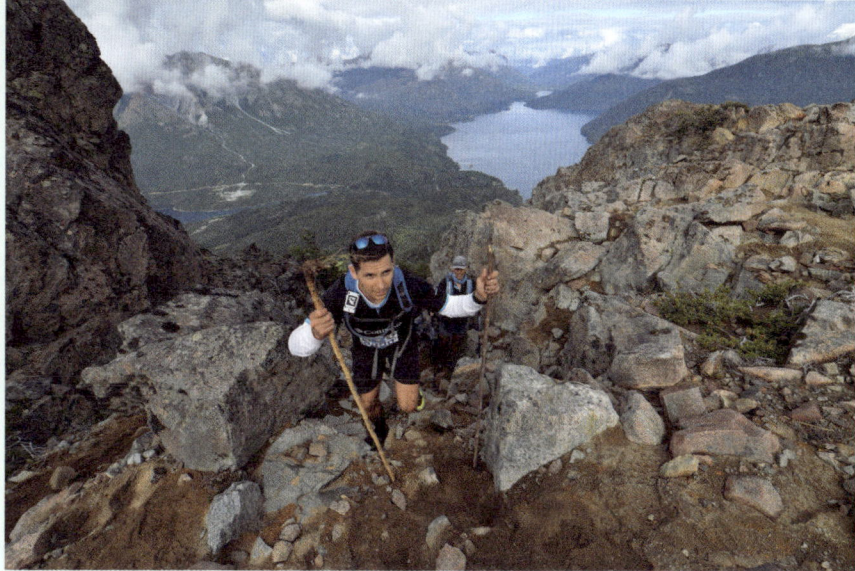

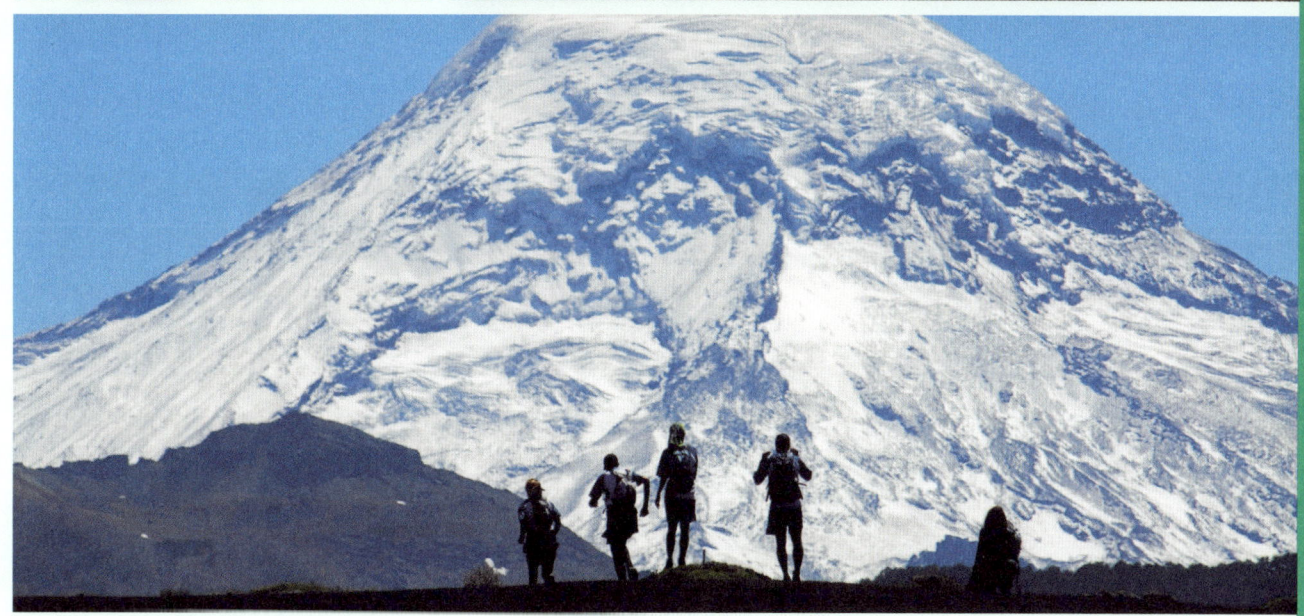

JOTIE

DO *you know where… your teenager is at five o'clock in… the morning?*
Young… people, things have… changed
Today the question for parents… is, it's ten a.m.
Do you know… where your children are?

Jump over fallen tree. Hard landing. Overload anti-shock memory.

…where… your teenager is at five o'clock in… the morning?

Dive under overhanging branch. Swish. Overload anti-shock memory, second time.

…drugs, dirty dancing and… pounding pounding techno music
We'll soon have you disco… dancing at the… discotheque

The Samantha Fu brothers are doing their best, but are not made for the nature trails of the Flemish Ardennes. For me too, it's improvising, but I absolutely wanted to run with music. My discman floats somewhere above my anal cleft, clamped behind the elastic straps of my boxer shorts and running trousers. My DJ headphones block out every trace of ambient noise. Or for as long

as my discman's anti-shock memory is ready to play ball.

Training for the college's annual cross-country. Soon we'll be served 3.8 field kilometres as a traditional exam. Why don't these PE teachers give us a training schedule? And why is it mandatory for all students, but with no imposed race for teaching staff? No idea how my condition is, because I hardly do any more karate. After seven years I'm tired of the endless technical series of kicks, thrusts and warding movements. Secretly, I'm just too scared to fight in competitions, where everyone is two heads taller than me. That broken ring finger from my last competition didn't help that fear one little bit.

A BROADER EXAMINATION OF THE SITUATION?

I traded scouting for Chiro because I didn't feel at home anymore. But that displaced the problem. My belly is a six-pack. Despite that, I'm jealous of my broad-shouldered classmates from the Latin-maths stream at my grammar school, where I ended up because I wanted to prove myself. My parents are both self-employed architects, often busy-busy-busy and therefore – without doubting their good intentions – not always present or near at hand. Probably they too would prefer it to be otherwise, but the train of life simply thunders on.

My father, just like his own father, is a much appreciated local politician, as a result of which I unwittingly get the identity of alderman's son. I used to read texts in the Sunday Mass, but I'm scarcely religious. I play rugby with the school team, but can't catch a ball. I DJ at parties, but am unable to *beatmix*. In between, I scratch away at texts for my high school's satirical student magazine. At home I regularly watch cycle racing with my father, I tease my sister and light fires with my brother in the back garden. On my bedside table is a book by guru Bhagwan Shree Rajneesh, underneath some pages from a sex book. Because I'm lost in the world, my mother introduces me with the best of intentions into an even larger world of esotericism. Because of this, I learn a degree of helplessness and end up in a dangerous pit of exaggerated contemplation. I wash it all through at class parties with lukewarm beer without a head.

In short: I'm a perfectly normal adolescent.

I turn into the forest proper. Away from the path. This is a nature reserve. No idea whether I'm trampling rare vegetation. I take a flashlight from my training jacket, because the dense vegetation hardly lets the pollution of light pass through. It's slithery. If I twist my foot here, it's going to be no fun hopping my way home. I told my mother I was going running, but not that I was going into the forest. My parents probably see this as dangerous, but I don't. When all's said and done, I've wandered all night long through forests in my youth movement, and this time the path is not littered with raped

wood nymphs or psychotic trolls. A trend that will probably continue for the rest of the route. Our national child murderer Marc Dutroux has been behind bars for four years. The likelihood that a colleague in oversized rubber boots will be lying in wait tonight with a chloroform rag is as good as zero.

And *Peetie-Loetie*?
   Couldn't he be waiting for me? My granny no doubt has other stories about this underworld figure with whom adults cooperate to get the kids off the street and into bed. In the meantime, I'm old enough to realize that this character exists only in fairy tales.

"Even though I'm just fifteen jogging minutes from home, the world seems very far away."

AM I GOING IN THE RIGHT DIRECTION?

I pause my discman and scan my surroundings with my flashlight. Even though I'm just fifteen jogging minutes from home, the world seems very far away. The foliage stifles the buzz of the constant traffic along the Scheldt valley. The smell of rotting leaves evokes the exquisite red wines that my maternal grandfather uncorks at family celebrations. Tonight, however, no silver candlesticks, only mud.

Château Rochecolombe seems to be located not in the Rhône valley, but in squelching Flemish mud. I push aside a set of branches and climb through a clump of thorn bushes to end up in a bowl-shaped meadow. When all of a sudden I hit this old rabbit warren. Now I'm back on the right track. The rising slope confirms my hypothesis. I bump over the sods and, at the end of the climb, plop down on the bench. I look out over the broad valley - a carpet of high-voltage cables, street lighting, parish churches, family houses and factories. 'It's quiet in all forests, lonely in all places', wrote local poet Jotie T'Hooft shortly before a cocaine overdose in 1977. Did he sit musing on this same bench? In the year 2000 I look a sissy in comparison with this famous neo-romantic social rebel. I don't care, because on this weekday night my micro adventure feels like a successful climb to the top of Mont Blanc.

Two weeks later, the starting shot of the field race will sound. Soured and out of breath, I'll end up just outside the top ten. Mission succeeded, no loss of face in front of the ladies who have shared our play-ground since the last school year. A break in a tradition established by nuns and priests. From now on muddy legs also without hairs.

▲▲▲

THE HOLY TRAIL

Scotland

SALOMON GLEN COE SKYLINE

52 KM | 34.2 MI • D+ 4,750 M | 15,584 FT

"If you build it, they will come... I have always loved that simple quote from the movie Field of Dreams. I had the same thought process when I started the Skyrunner National Series in the UK. I was told: Skyrunning in the UK, don't be silly. It's not possible."

Ian Corless
WWW.IANCORLESS.ORG

DAD

"**PFFF,** I'm going for a walk..."
"You're not, are you?
Come on!"
"Yes... to be able to drink better."
"OK, but after taking on supplies, run again!"
"Yes, Yes…"

It's easy to talk from astride my mountain bike, but I do have the right to speak. Last year I ran a marathon for the first time. Today my father is running the same route. Like me, he's chosen Luxembourg's Echternach Marathon for his defloration. The race has two laps around the lake and two turning points in the valley. The whole surrounded by wooded hills to which this region owes its unofficial name of Little Switzerland.

My father throws his empty cup into the garbage bag.
"*Allez*! And now run again!"

At home there's a divorce in the making, but I've not cottoned onto that yet. With my brother and sister at the arrival, these last kilometres are pure father-son. A new perspective: I point the way and he follows. Beyond the short sentences we exchange, for the first time in a long time I feel more connected than average to him. Because we are on the road together again? Does the key lie in his current vulnerability? Or does it have to do with the running itself?
"Yes, Yes…"
"At the bridge in the distance, it's still 3 kilometres to go!"
"Yes, Yes…"

I still remember the benchmark from last year. There I met the 'man with the hammer', but I keep that memory to myself today. Touch wood he doesn't go for my father this year.

STUDENT

In my head, I go back over how I found myself on the starting line last year. As a first-year student in Germanic Languages it had been a changeable year. I drowned like a rookie in the end-of-year exam system, lost my way in syntax and stumbled over sound shifts. I needed a boost before starting History with my exemptions. Don't ask me how or why, but suddenly I was faced with the challenge of running from my hometown in East Flanders to Ostend. I did go jogging regularly, but for 70 kilometres in two days, and despite my youthful condition, low body weight and total naivety it seemed a good idea to go looking for advice. I knocked on the door of a running friend of my father. He first had a good laugh at my project, suggested that I first try an ordinary marathon and referred me to the Sports Medicine department of the Ghent University Hospital for an exercise test on the treadmill. From the professors I received a twelve-week training schedule, which I followed for only nine weeks. Not out of unfaithfulness, but because *Le Marathon Vert de Echternach* - a must according to my father's friend - took place in nine weeks.

"Come on, Dad! Doing well!"

YOUNG MR BEER-BELLY

In the end I did it in 3 hours and 25 minutes as the youngest participant, surprising not only my father's friend, but also myself. After that, the academic year started, which this time I got through successfully. However, there were no further running exploits. I was young and had seen enough asphalt disappear under my legs. The belly with which I'm sitting on the bike today is the logical result.

Hey, you there…
   What was your name again?
   Right, yes.
   Young Mr Beer-Belly!
   Nice, a little cycling, don't you think?

"With my brother and sister at the arrival, these last kilometres are pure father-son. A new perspective: I point the way and he follows."

Actually, I'm anything but a history freak. The dinner the day before yesterday among fellow students was fortunately freaky enough to compensate for the difference in historical knowledge. The hangover is still spinning in my body. How else could it be? Glasses of red wine on a base of cheese fondue - *La Grande Bouffe* in the superlative - in my student room. For dessert there were corks that we held in the flames of the candles. With the soot we daubed each other's faces until we were in fits of laughter. My father is too much in *the death zone* to read the inner fun of this memory from my face. I hear him puffing beside me.
   "Still OK?"
   "I'll be happy when I get there!"
   "Another 2 kilometres! You're almost there!"

Not much later a signaller forbids me to ride on, because the path narrows and the rows of spectators are becoming denser. I quickly get onto the main road and rush to my brother and sister, who are at the finishing line. Not much later we shout our father on to finish his marathon. 42 kilometres in 4 hours and 2 minutes.

I stretch my back, run my hands through my hair and crave a cigarette. ▲▲▲

USA

BARKLEY MARATHONS

**Trail fighting is perhaps
a better term for this race.**

Wartburg
BARKLEY MARATHONS

5 x ±32-42km | 20-26mi
D+ 16,500m | 54,133ft

- ⊕ Anything but open to all
- ⊕ Unique
- ⊕ 101 surreal rituals

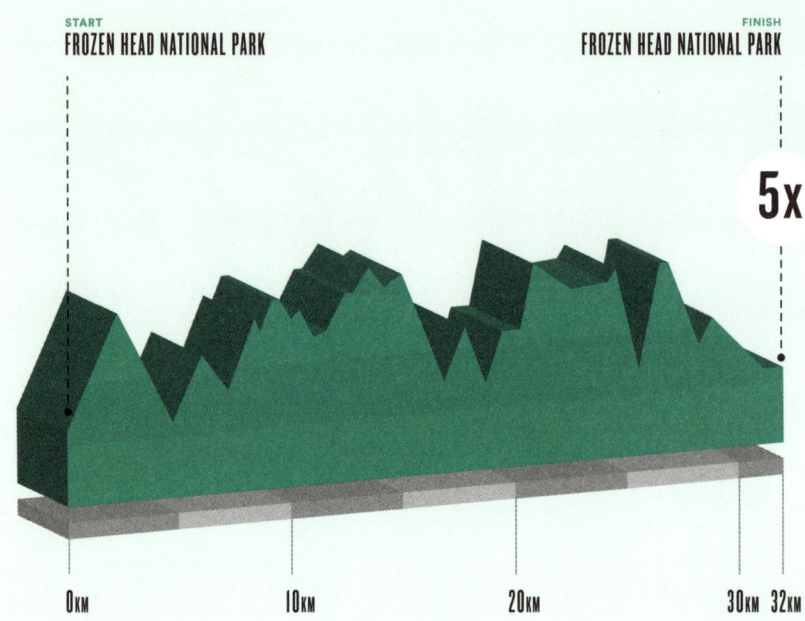

START
FROZEN HEAD NATIONAL PARK

FINISH
FROZEN HEAD NATIONAL PARK

5x

0km   10km   20km   30km 32km

MICHIEL PANHUYSEN

Age 50 • Author
The Hague • Netherlands

Why did you choose this race?

MICHIEL "Man in his pride selects his own challenges, but not so in this competition. It's like buying a house... If you want a place to live, you go looking. Usually, you don't immediately find what you want. Until you give up and unexpectedly a house turns up. A dream house you fall in love with and that you have to buy. The asking price is far too high, but you sign the deed. In love too it can sometimes be like that: if you search, you won't find it either. Love overwhelms you when you least expect it. In this way too, Barkley chooses you. Also the registration procedure is secret.

But if you belong there, then this is not an obstacle. This is the only race that chooses you and not the other way around."

How did you prepare?

MICHIEL "I didn't know what was coming. You just do your mileage, as you do for every long race. I decided to go up a hill once in a while - something I never did otherwise. I was also careful to combine all kinds of efforts. Both power training and uphill runs. Long training sessions and fast intervals. I didn't really care about choice of equipment. For me it makes no difference whether I run in cheap Kalenji shoes, or the latest S-Lab Salomon running suit. It's much more important to prepare yourself mentally. In any event, it's a big misunderstanding that a race should be fun. Something like 'nice, huh!'... Not so. But to transcend that, you have to appeal to something higher. If you believe in God, it's simple. If, like me, you don't, then you have to appeal to something higher in yourself. But to whom or what exactly? These were the sort of questions I was asking myself without knowing it. For example, the Barkley Marathons don't offer medical support. There are no manned aid stations out there. There's no rescue service. You have to be prepared for this kind of loneliness and uncertain circumstances. Many people take up running too light-heartedly. For example, they train in good weather. But you can also go looking for difficulties. For example, you can't wait until that downpour is over, but consciously choose to go out in pouring rain. It's simply all about your attitude to life. In my experience, running an ultra-trail is going looking for what happens on that other, unknown side. It simply comes down to training for something that will present itself without your having control over it."

How did your race go?

MICHIEL "I've taken part four times. My first time in 2012, I ran an entire round behind Frozen Ed, a legendary Barkley veteran. That's how I got to know the route a bit. On my

Race director Lazarus 'Laz' Lake named his race after his neighbour and former racer Barry Barkley. To return the compliment, Barry delivers hundreds of chicken drumsticks every year to the Barkley tent camp. The entire stock of Barkleychicken goes frozen onto the barbecue during the race. A delicacy eaten charred on the outside and red-raw on the inside. For real men (and women) only!

second time I went into the woods alone. Very exciting, but also overwhelming and scary. I decided to stop and wait for other runners. I then held out for half a round, until I was completely broken. I'd never run for more than 24 hours. In particular I realized then that I wasn't ready for it mentally. The following two years it was each time the same recipe: the first round and a part of the second round. 20 to 24 hours on the road and gouging in the dense fog until you encounter your own footsteps in the snow. In 2016, I finally succeeded in finishing two rounds. At that time I was in a very good shape, but I just came in at the last minute. It was a few minutes before the cut-off time, but I had no energy or mental strength for a following round. In theory, I could have quickly stuffed food and drinks in my backpack and rested half an hour in the grass after the start of my third round. But I didn't

do it. Why? Yes, why?... Let's just say that a third round would have cost me at least another 24 hours. In this way, I lost my chance for the Fun Run. I'm still thinking about it, but maybe I'll try again this year."

Which moment will you never forget?

MICHIEL "I could write a book about it - which I'm currently doing. It's difficult to choose a specific moment. All the moments that I think of have the same thing in common. The Barkley is an intimate family reunion with lots of loved ones. I'm thinking, for example, of Stuart Glemann. A veteran with very crazy stories about spaceships, but what a special man! He's now dead, but I hung onto his lips for hours. Did you know that the medicine men of the original US population prohibited their tribe from entering the Barkley area? Too dangerous, they said.

THE HOLY TRAIL

"Not All Pain is Gain."

The forest was supposed to be in the grip of dark magnetic fields... The reason for this race was the escape of James Earl Ray, the murderer of Martin Luther King Jr., from the prison in the middle of the forest. His story fits perfectly with this mythology. He was free for 55 hours, but covered just 13 kilometres. How does that happen? There are lots of blackberry bushes, but surely you can skirt around them? Spirits are not my thing, but just too often weird things happen in that forest. For example, one moment there's not a breath of wind, and the next there's a whirlwind next to you. Or your compass suddenly goes crazy and points south instead of north. Are those hallucinations from lack of sleep or is the Barkley just an elongated creepy fairy tale? You'll not find these kinds of stories in the classic race reports. I've no idea whether this is reality or fantasy, but these kinds of testimonies are part of the bigger Barkley picture."

A golden tip for future participants?

MICHIEL "Yes, absolutely: stay away! (laughs). Ah, the Barkley is simply an impossible task. More for dowsers than for trail runners, in fact. Since the 2014 Netflix documentary about the race, it's full of journalists reporting live on the race. Pathetic how they stand there screaming at that yellow barrier! But I understand why Laz lets them. The nature reserve in which the Barkley takes place can use media attention. It brings money to the region. As a result, Laz gains credit from the park rangers in order to be allowed to continue the race at all. It's about give and take. And that includes tension and polemics. Laz knows better than anyone how to play things off against each other. For example, it's possible there'll be no new Barkley this or next year, that the race disappears just like that. Laz is also no longer the youngest, you know. His dream is to walk right across America, as a kind of final life project. He's not going to wait years for that..."

BELGICANO

Jesus Christ! After a handful of runs it's clear: that marathon is now a really long way off. My lungs feel like a clogged vacuum cleaner. By extension, an inflated balloon through all the combinations of sugar and alcohol I've absorbed over the last few months in this city. And those *pintxos* - the Basque tapas with their distinctive toothpick that holds everything together.

Hello, young master Beer-Belly! Clearly you enjoy being in Spain, huh! And how large you've become...

"It's Mr Beer-Belly!"

"What did you say?"

"You understood me well."

"Do you really mean that? Gosh yeah... If you really want to; I'm not stopping you."

"Absolutely! From now on, my name's no longer young master Beer-Belly; but Mr Beer-Belly. Or *señor Panza*, as they say here."

"Sancho Panza?"

"No, you idiot! He goes with Don Quixote. My name is *SEÑOR PANZA*!"

"Steady on, mate..."

"Or MR BEER-BELLY! Fix it well between your ears, OK!?"

THE SOUND OF MUSIC

The headache is retreating, but my brain is still only half functioning. What happened last night falls into the category of *Things the grandchildren should know*. To celebrate six months' Erasmus in Bilbao, I took my laptop, records and CDs with me. Every two weeks I DJ in one club or another, accompanied or not with pole dancers. I still cannot *beatmix*, but take advantage of the Spanish musical landscape. In Belgium meanwhile, under the influence of 2many-djs, it's *bon ton* to mix different genres and style periods. For that you need some musical background, and a bit of courage, instead of seamlessly playing one CD after another. Clubs and bars here tend to stick with the genre that they've chosen for their nightly den. Despite my miserable DJ abilities, my encyclopaedic pinball machine exudes an exoticism that Basque night ravens seem to appreciate.

Yesterday I was programmed as the closing event in a youth club. Well, 'youth club': a *gaztetxea*, mid-way between a squat and a left-nationalist party office. On my first visit, my eye immediately fell on the photos above the counter. Views of unshaven men and women, who used to be associated with the ETA and are currently rotting in state prisons in the far south of Spain. It was then that I got talking with two local radio DJs. Would I like to DJ at their party next weekend? Of course! What they didn't tell me at the time was that their radio programme was 95% about the self-cultivation of marijuana.

Fifteen minutes before it was my turn, I blew in. A nod to the DJ duo with dreadlocks, whose Jamaican tunes like a slow metronome provided the crowded youth house with bass sounds. I dropped my things next to their CD bags. One of the two local radio DJs gave me my *pocket money* for this evening. To be paid in drink vouchers and a bag of marijuana? It was something unique in my career, but it was nothing compared to what I saw in the audience. Large dishes with thick buds of marijuana were passing from hand to hand. Artfully created joints, which origami enthusiasts and model builders would be proud of: rolled rockets, mushrooms and tulips.

The order of the day turned out to be less rosy. The dreadlocked DJs had to be up early the next day and took their turntable with them. I had to make do with a bric-à-brac mixing board for video images, a DVD player, a cheap stereo chain and a micro. In a panic I was looking for a socket for my headphones, only to decide a few seconds later that pre-listening the songs would not be for this lot.

How did I end up here? Was I here as *El Belgicano* – a nickname I'd received from my professor of *Antropología Histórica* – as headliner or after party? And what music exactly does a person put on after an evening of

perfectly mixed reggae, dub and ska? "Stick to your trade," my grandmother would have replied - in line with the teasing reply when I called her a month ago, because I wanted to make Flemish stew in grandmother's way for my Erasmus friends.

"If I go out and dance long enough, do I become a good runner again?"

Gradually I got into my pace. The carbon monoxide in my blood made way for oxygen. On the other side of the winding Nervión, the titanium cover plates of the Guggenheim shine out. I've lived here long enough to know the different forms of the building. Dull and expressionless in clouds, a mirror-smooth diamond in rain and fire and flames in low sun. A modern cathedral, where docks and workers' houses still stood a decade ago. My body also could use a make-over. The sweat pours from my body. Just like tonight, when with trembling hands I put on 'Monstertruckdriver' by the German one-man wonder T.Raumschmiere as an opening track. Sink or swim. Preferring the second scenario, I pull off my T-shirt, throw the micro into the crowd and boldly turn the volume tiles of the mixing console.

THIS IS NOT BORN TO RUN, BUT BORN TO DANCE.

A stray, totally-smashed punk caught the micro in spite of his half litre of *kalimoxo* and shouted his soul out of his body to the digital WOO-OOO-OOO OO-OO. Green Velvet, Daft Punk, Tiga or Beastie Boys? 'La Rock', the stamper by Vitalic? Or something more Belgian with 'Push' by Universal? Between the shrill bells and the booming groove, I finally mixed my favourite number by French techno jazz king Laurent Garnier. With his slower 'The Sound of the Big Babou' I switched back for my drug-high audience, to pour more oil on the fire. Into the beatless intermezzo I thrust the most recognizable drumbeat of the 1990s:

Woo-hoo
When I feel heavy-metal
And I'm pins and I'm needles
Well, I lie and I'm easy
All the time but I am never sure
Why I need you
Pleased to meet you

I search for the song on my mp3 player and enjoy. Before I realize it, I feel the same vibe and energy as tonight. Maybe running and dancing are brother and sister? In recent months, I trained especially in the last discipline, in front of and behind the mixer, mostly out of the beat.

If I go out and dance long enough, do I become a good runner again? ▲▲▲

Italy

THE NORTH FACE

LAVAREDO ULTRA TRAIL

See it as a long day's outing.

Cortina d'Ampezzo
CORTINA TRAIL

48km | 30mi • D+ 2,600m | 8,530ft

- ⊕ The majestic Drei Zinnen aka Tre Cime di Lavaredo (on the path of The North Face® Lavaredo Ultra Trail)
- ⊕ Rough terrain from erosion and weathering
- ⊕ At least as beautiful as the UTMB®, they say

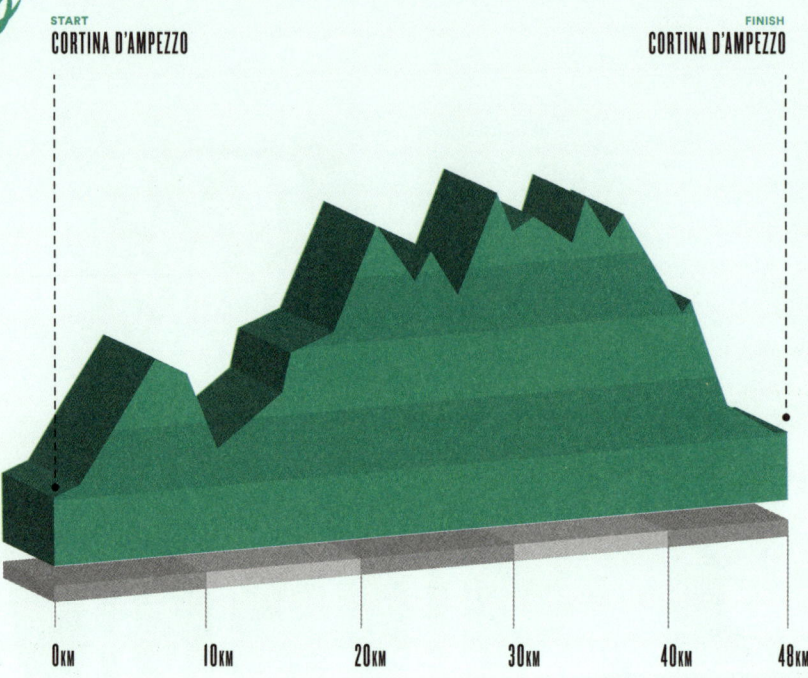

START
CORTINA D'AMPEZZO

FINISH
CORTINA D'AMPEZZO

0KM 10KM 20KM 30KM 40KM 48KM

OTHER DISTANCES

CORTINA SKYRACE
20km | 12.5mi • D+ 1,000m | 3,281ft

THE NORTH FACE® LAVAREDO ULTRA TRAIL
120km | 74.5mi • D+ 5,800m | 19,209ft

ANNA EDWARD

Age 46 • Rental manager
Pollença, Mallorca • Spain

Why did you choose this race?

ANNA "A few years ago, I was in the Dolomites for my work and found it beautiful at the time. But in the end, it was a video of the event on Facebook that intrigued me. That landscape, with those three iconic rock towers of the Drei Zinnen as icing on the cake. Friends told me that for them this event was more beautiful than the Ultra-Trail du Mont-Blanc®, because the terrain is so rough. I love running because it makes me happy and allows me to enjoy spectacular landscapes. So yes, into the Dolomites! I'd done 100 kilometres on the Camí de Cavalls, a GR route on Menorca, in 14 hours. 48 kilometres in Italy should also work, shouldn't it?"

How did you prepare?

ANNA "By way of preparation, I ran about 60 kilometres a week. Not too much really for such an intense trail race, but at my age I have to pay extra attention to injuries. That's why I held back a bit. Sometimes by alternating running and walking, sometimes by diving into the gym for circuit training. Consistent stretching and stability training with Pilates. In this way, you use your entire body, with the least risk of overloading it. When running, I talk constantly with running buddies.

This is to make sure I don't run too fast. I have to keep my head. I once sprained my ankle while running from having my eyes too much on the landscape and not enough on the trail. Good for four no-running months on doctor's orders. Now I can laugh at it, but at the time it was a minor drama."

How did your race go?

ANNA "I thought that after those 100 kilometres on Menorca I was a mountain runner, but I had to revise my ideas. Our highest mountain on Majorca is just 1,445 metres high. Those Dolomites are really in a different class. A 600-metre climb right at the start. An immediate wake-up call that there was serious work ahead. I thought I was going fast, but that was just an illusion. Everyone crawled up in slow motion, me too. After a small descent, you immediately had the longest climb of the day. About 1,000 metres up, if I'm not mistaken, to Col de Bois. Firm climbing, with some snow here and there. I remember well that I was afraid of altitude sickness. If you live close to the sea, like me, then you really feel the difference in oxygen. I didn't make very fast time, and was afraid of missing the cut-off time on Passo Giau. Eventually I succeeded, but the real sting was in the tail. The last 10 kilometres are downhill, but it's no gift. The path is strewn with tree roots and therefore very technical. I caught a cramp in my leg and fell. Fortunately,

Race secret

The logo of this race depicts the triple peak of the Drei Zinnen, aka Tre Cime di Lavaredo. As the double name suggests, this mountaintop lies on the border between German-speaking Austria and Italian-speaking (how could it be otherwise?) Italy. Historical fact: the Grosse Zinne or Cima Grande is the highest of this iconic trio at 2,999 metres. During the First World War, the Italian army exploited this fact, placing a battery of spotlights to check what their Austrian neighbours were doing at night. The corridors carved into the flanks of these peaks remain as silent reminders of this military sentry post. Mind you, the spotlights have disappeared. Participants in the longest distance: please don't leave your headlamps at home.

I had a spray to deal with the pain. This allowed me to continue after a few minutes and I finished the race. All's well that ends well, because I don't like giving up. I was a bit tired, but I wasn't fully aware of it. It was just a long day's outing (laughs). I started running only six years ago and finally I could call myself a mountain runner. Although I'm not a school model. For example, I had running sticks, but I didn't use them once. Nor am I a typical runner in terms of nutrition. Those dry cookies in the aid stations or the energy gels some trail racers rely on? Ugh! I can never swallow them. So I had sandwiches, Snickers and M&Ms in my backpack. Maybe I sound more like a running candy shop than a mountain runner, but it works for me."

Which moment will you never forget?

ANNA "I'm not a competition beast, but some men clearly didn't like my overtaking them (laughs). Southern temperament, no doubt?"

A golden tip for future participants?

ANNA "During the race, try to run alongside positive people. Good vibes are just as important as a good condition!"

"Probably the most beautiful race I have ever run."

Anton Krupicka

SCREEN WORKER

"**NUTTER!**" "Sexy outfit!"
"Off running
again?"
"Don't forget to clock out!"
"Full thrust! I'll join you next time!"
"Something went wrong in my knee while running last weekend. What can I do about it?"

The policy of the government agency I work for is top-down, strict and sometimes vague. With all its paradoxes, food for never-ending discussions at lunch, unless, that is, you go your own way at noon. To avoid the constantly-recurring spectrum of comments from colleagues in the lift on my running gear, I've started taking the fire escape with the shyness of an Afghan sniper. *Skyscraper running*, but in reverse.

The twenty-floor descent has more to do with gravity than with physical strength. Within two months I'll be running the 20 km through Brussels with colleagues. To increase my chances of success, I've quit smoking for the third time. If you feel that you need your lungs, you'll see the value of maintaining them properly.

Honest?
It sucks.

MR BEER-BELLY

In my mind I'm still the marathon runner of Echternach, but my whole body contradicts that. I'm a fat ox and am ashamed of the amount of fat protruding above my running pants.

Hi, Mr Beer-Belly, *long time no see*!

I lost sight of you on the way to Nepal. Yes, I know. That trip was not for you, hitchhiking through low-alcohol Muslim countries. Far too many skipped meals and eternally lugging that mess of a backpack. Not to mention the 250 km hiking through the Himalayas.

Sorry…

And Mr Beer-Belly, what have you been doing in the meantime?

Glad to be back?

Dura lex, sed lex. It's not enough to think you're a runner. Or to dream about it. Or to pretend to be one. Finally, you have to tie those running shoes - again and again. Starting running again is first of all accepting that you can no longer do it. Previous battles won are just memories, the plastic medals from various city runs in the corner of my desk at home no more than silent witnesses that I once moved.

"It's not enough to think you're a runner."

Between the fifteenth and fourteenth floors I insert my earphones to block the sound of my own puffing. I press 'play' and bump into British techno from my puberty. This morning I shuffled into my employer's office with the second double espresso of the day.

You got a velvet mouth
You're so succulent and beautiful
Shimmering and dirty
Wonderful and hot times.

The sweat beads from my forehead when, at the end of the stairs, I blow through the revolving door and dive down the escalator to the outer door. The drizzle is a welcome refreshment. Staircases are not cool river gorges in oxygen-rich primeval forests.

PHYSICS

Before changing, I bumped on Facebook into a few films from the American production house Duct Tape Then Beer. In one of their commercials for the Arc'teryx outdoor brand, a 46-year-old father appears. He confesses that he eats too many fries and knocks back too much beer. He too, I chuckle. He's prouder of the moments he spends outdoors, with burning lungs gasping for air. In contrast to the exotic advertising film, in this office district you cannot boulder, ice climb, mountain bike or ski. Nonetheless, his attitude to life makes sense: "We're all trying to be busy instead of living. We shift data on our computers, while we'd be better shifting ourselves. I know it's hard, but vegetating in a seat should not be the rule, but a satisfying change. Pure physics: a moving object tends to stay in motion. The more often you sit, the more effort it takes to get moving. The less you move... Well, you've got the picture. Move. Move faster. Move against gravity to avoid being sucked into the pit."

Shouting lager lager lager lager
Mega mega white thing
Mega mega white thing
So many things to see and do.

I'm a bureaucratic computer worker. For the first time in my life I'm in a permanent job. Hurrah?

Financially, certainly. In addition, the large group of young colleagues gives a sense of stability after numerous fill-in assignments in education, internships as a copywriter and editor and writing a book about my trip to Nepal. Office number 2010, where I've been working for a few years now, has an almost domestic stability. It's one of the beacons that help me keep my life together after the disintegration of the litter I grew up in.

How alert should I be? Who can be trusted? Rest or keep moving? Run or run away?

LION OR GAZELLE

A second short film by Duct Tape Then Beer that I've just seen floats through my head: "As a child, my father often told me this story. He said that the gazelle woke up every morning knowing that it would have to run faster that day than the fastest lion so as not to end up as his snack. But the lion also woke up every morning, my father said. And the lion knew that he had to run faster that day than the slowest gazelle in order not to go hungry. Then my father always asked me the same question: are you the lion or the gazelle? I never had an answer ready."

Am I a lion? Or a gazelle?

Actually, I succeed only 50% in doing my job properly. I score well on the human part, but far too often I stumble over the administrative and bureaucratic nature of my day job. Nevertheless, I do my best, but I'm losing all my fire. My talents are elsewhere, but you don't leave just like that a golden cage that is now a warm nest of colleagues.

"We're all running. Some are running away from something - others are running towards something. We love the heavy kilometres, but also the light ones. 100,000 km brought you to the run you're doing now, the next run to 1,000 future runs. The sun rises and sets. Meanwhile, we continue running. Through the years I learned that it's not all about the race, but about running itself. I know that my mind is stronger than the rocks that I run over. I bow, but will not break. I'm an animal in these mountains. Whether I'm a lion or a gazelle? The answer doesn't matter. When the sun comes up, they both run."

Hi mom are you having fun
And now are you on your way
To a new tension
headache.

Meanwhile, the office towers of Brussels' Northern District are behind me. As a child I swore never to work in such an aquarium, and now I'm right there. Life sometimes demands compromises in order to make other pathways possible.

At the Petit Château, I pound against the wind, which has free play along the canal. I wisely alternate running and walking.

Keeping moving?
Work hard, play hard?
FOMO – Fear of Missing Out?
YOLO – You Only Live Once?

At Saint-Jean-Molenbeek, the right bank of the canal becomes African-coloured. Customers ponder hard before buying second cars which they will load full and cross with to the black continent. Loudly negotiating men and theatricals that end in a handshake and a pile of banknotes. I shuffle along on my bare, pale legs.

AGAIN A FLASH FROM DUCT TAPE THEN BEER

In their clip *Silence*, a man in a suit dabs at his computer screen. A thumping stapler and nervously ringing telephone form the recurring soundtrack of his existence, interrupted only by a pleading piano chord that pops up every time he dons his running shoes. Silence and space to breathe. After the shower the carousel beckons again. He sighs, but duty calls. Until you suddenly see an empty office chair, which is spinning as if someone just jumped out of it. In the next shot you don't see the office slave any more, but you hear him. His gently crunching running steps announce him, until he comes into view round the corner on a mountain path. Instead of the dull expression on his face you now read serenity that turns into childish wonder and ecstasy at the view of the mountain in the rising morning sun.

Life is full of noise. Do we still know how silence sounds?

In Anderlecht I pushed myself over the bridge. The other bank is more coffee-coloured. Shops with water pipes and tajine dishes. The largest number of kebab shops per inhabitant in Belgium. A *hellhole*, according to an orange president. Strange how this canal in this metropolis acts at once as a natural and a cultural boundary.

We doesn't exist without the *other*?

"Life is full of noise. Do we still know how silence sounds?"

Back in the North District I call the lift to the twentieth floor. I'm not taking the fire escape to the twentieth floor. Meanwhile, in my head, I run over the file that I want to finish this afternoon. Arguments back and forth. And then decide, because *nous sommes quand même confrontés avec une situation de crise and l'influx reste quand même signifiant.*

After a quick shower, I push down a sandwich in front of my computer. A new e-mail: "Friday beers soon in Flamingo?"

Reply: *"Of course!"*
Mr Beer-Belly, are you coming?
"Guess so!" ▲▲▲

France
MARATHON
DU
MONT-BLANC

5 TRAIL RACES

"When I finally
reach the top my
mum is waiting at
the aid station and
is almost surprised
to see me coming so
early. Obviously the
last time she saw
me I was about to
collapse from low
blood sugar."

Michael Carraz

WWW.ULTRARUNNINGCOMMUNITY.COM

INFLAMMATION

I open the door to my physiotherapist's office. By now, I know the ritual. Undress and onto the treatment table.
"How were the exercises that I gave you?"
"Hmm..."

At the counter at home, on the station platform and at the copying machine at work: standing on one leg and seeking balance, one foot crossed over the other and bending sideways, stretching the calves on a step.

Together with my physiotherapist and *Doctor Google,* I do everything I can to fight the inflamed tendons in my body: a long dormant tendon inflammation in both heels and an acute right *runner's knee.*

Plantar fasciitis and iliotibial friction syndrome.

ANOTHER ROUND

The first condition is best described as two thumbtacks onto which you step when getting out of bed on the wrong side in the morning. The second as a Five Point Palm Exploding Heart Technique on your knee.

Both injuries are a result of overload.

I've been in a running club since the 20 km and have driven up my mileage too quickly. In a youth movement for adults it's at times difficult to say no with a rediscovered running virus and naive enthusiasm - especially if you don't yet know your own boundaries.

"Saturday we're going to a race. Are you coming?"
"YES!"
"Another round?"
"YES!"

Today as the first course of the menu: proprioceptive neuromuscular fascination.
"Proprio-what?"
"A stretch technique, because your legs are incredibly stiff! You really need to stretch more after exercise. Or yoga, that would be good for you too."

After he's stretched my frame one hundredth of a millimetre longer, it's time for the big work. He gestures me to lie down on my side. From the previous treatment session, I know what comes next.

From his desk he takes an object that is midway between an antique doorknob and a child's top. The convex side disappears in his palm. With the blunted point he seeks out the over-stretched tendon between my knee and pelvis. I jump from the pain, but let him complete his praxis. Ironing folds flat requires effort, also with the body.

"You're slightly knock-kneed."

"Oh, if you say so?"

"This automatically gives you more tension on the outside of your knee."

"That explains a lot."

"And you turn your foot inwards as you move forward. Overpronation is what it's called. This places additional stress on your knee from below. Have you already thought of insoles?"

Knock-knees, insoles, inflammations?

Maybe man is not *Born to Run,* as McDougall suggests in his book about the Tarahumara. As a journalist-runner he immersed himself in this primitive tribe, where even the wiriest elderly people seemed able to run incredibly long distances. How did his theory go?

JURASSIC

The mystery of these running Indians made anthropologists look back to prehistoric times, McDougall argues. Four million years ago, the brains of the humanoid australopithecus were the same size as a pea. Two million years later there was the homo erectus with the brain volume of a melon.

Such physiological development requires concentrated energy, according to McDougall. In other words, meat had to come on the table to feed this growth.

The corner butcher's shop didn't yet exist. Nor did man yet have the intelligence to produce sharp weapons. This we succeeded in doing only 200,000 years ago. A small calculation shows that the first people successfully hunted for 1.8 million years without weapons. A bizarre fact, because without claws or tusks, we were the sissies of the jungle. Man has hardly any power or speed compared to his prey. Speaking of humiliation: even a tiny squirrel is faster than a seasoned runner.

So how did we get to those juicy ribs and tender haunches?

In evolutionary terms, we have one huge advantage over all other mammals: we can cool off damn well by sweating. An antelope or a deer does not sweat. They always have to choose: to run away or to cool with the mouth wide open. The two together are physically impossible. Man exploited this advantage of moving smoothly under a leaden sun: for 1.8 million years we remained hard on the heels of our prey until they were exhausted.

Man was born as a runner, but has lost the scent since domestication.

All well and good, but why as a runner do I lie in the rag basket, dear McDougall? Can you explain that to me, friend?

The author is resolute. Running shoes are cages that reduce the natural springing effect of the bed of our feet. As a result, we run unnaturally and our body is distorted. The solution?

Get rid of Nike, Adidas and Asics!

LONG LIVE BAREFOOT RUNNING!

My physiotherapist shakes his head: "It's not that simple. You've been running in shoes all your life. As soon as you started to walk, your parents wrapped these things round you. Your footbed has become so lazy that you would get extra injuries very quickly if you now switch to barefoot running. Switching has to be done very gradually. Try to alternate as much as possible. Walking barefoot at home. Sometimes with insoles in your shoes, sometimes not. And build up gently again, got it?"
  "Yes, Yes…"

I nod, but have not heard the last sentence. Running is my new drug, which gives me structure and meaning. Instead of visiting the pub with friends, I now more often run off the day. Endorphins, dopamine, serotonin and adrenalin instead of a pint. The mix of camaraderie, excitement and euphoria at the finish completes the strong cocktail.

Addictions grow with time. What if I'm unable to run regularly? To admit to myself that the opposite of addiction is connecting with others?

"And try to pay attention to your diet. Those excess kilos are not helping you recover. Extra weight means extra impact and stress on your frame."
  Satisfied now, Mr Beer-Belly? And wipe that grin off your face! ▲▲▲

USA

LEADVILLE
TRAIL 100
RUN

Llamas in a far too long cowboy movie!

Colorado
LEADVILLE TRAIL 100 RUN

160km | 100mi
D+ 5,000m | 16,404ft

- American spirit!
- High cowboy content
- In between Hardrock 100 and the Western States Endurance Run

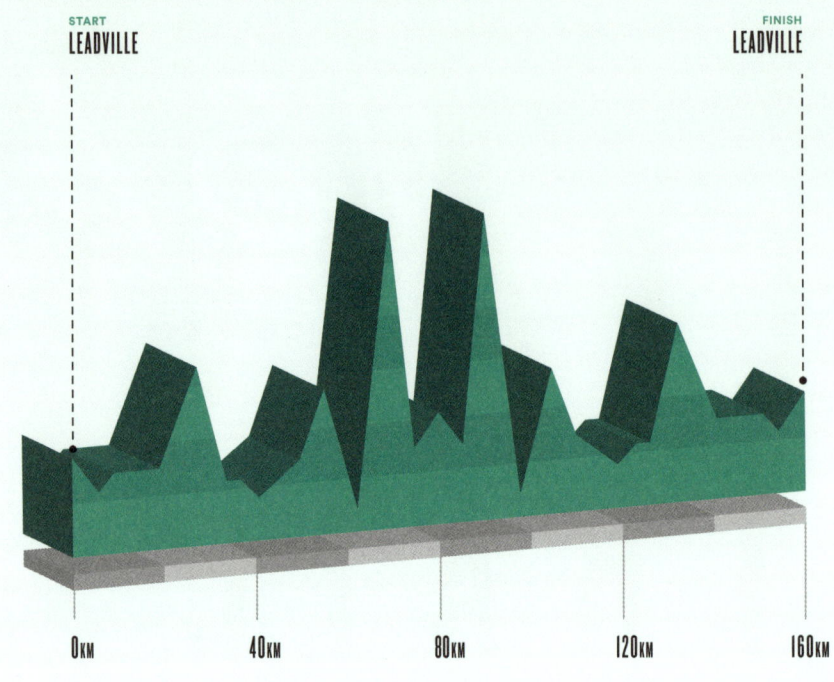

START
LEADVILLE

FINISH
LEADVILLE

0km   40km   80km   120km   160km

MARC WEENING

Age 40 • Entrepreneur
Doorwerth • Netherlands

Why did you choose this race?

MARC "I'd been trail running in the Low Countries for eight years and dreamed of doing a 100 miler. With The Great Escape, The Bello Gallico and the Legends Trail, you have a few super-long races in the Belgian Ardennes, but I didn't want to run in my backyard. 100 miles or 160 kilometres is very long, and for that, I wanted new terrain. I found inspiration in the legendary *Born to Run* book, which had originally prompted me to make trail running a bigger part of my life. In that book, the Tarahumara leave their Mexican canyon to take part in Leadville, a classic American

100-miler in Colorado. That's how I heard about this race for the first time and it stuck. I also noticed that there's a lot that blows over from the USA. A large part of the product development takes place there and you have a heap of magazines dedicated specifically to our sport. But I especially wanted to experience that culture and scene for myself. Initially I also thought of the Hardrock 100 and the Western States Endurance Run. These iconic 100 milers are often mentioned in the same breath as Leadville. Hardrock also takes place in Colorado, but has extremely stiff registration conditions and few entry tickets. The chance of getting an entry ticket is minimal, nothing you can base any plans on. The Western States in California is the world's oldest 100 miler with a fantastic history, but a lot flatter and technically less interesting than Hardrock and Leadville. That way I came back to my original inspiration. The story of the race itself also appealed to me tremendously. In the early 1980s, the mine closed and the mountain village was flooded with unemployment. Unlike other villages in the area, Leadville is not a ski resort with shit-chic hotels generating tourist dollars. In order to survive, the former miners decided to play on the charm and authentic character of their western village in order to attract cash. In those days, it was also questionable whether it was possible to complete such a long race at high altitudes. It seemed really exotic to me to go trail running in the setting of a cowboy film."

How did you prepare?

MARC "Hours and hours of running. Also lots of cycling. And hiking, putting the kids in the backpack and trudging uphill. Pure power training! The first steps were unconsciously a few 50 milers I'd done in the years before my registration. For the first time you experience these nagging aches. In your knees, your back, your feet. But you learn to deal with them. You've learned that they can also pass. Through experience, you know that pain you have counted with

Race secret

There are no helicopters in Leadville. The locals use llamas for transport in the mountains, because these animals are excellent at high altitudes. This way you immediately know how aid stations are supplied. And you can reassure yourself during the race: you're not hallucinating and you've not run off-track into the Andes!

is not a breaking point, but something that you have to learn to embrace. Of course, I surfed the internet to get a clear picture of the race. Not only through YouTube films and *race reports*, but also through contact with other trail runners. For example, I skyped with two locals who know the race and the area through and through. In this way I built up a picture and knew what was in store for me. In terms of footwear, I had to think for a bit, because having the right shoes for such long distances is a story on its own. Leadville has a number of river passages, so wet shoes are guaranteed. Your feet swell, so you may have to deal with blisters and sodden feet. To avoid this, I chose shoes with extra toe space. That's how I ended up with the Altra brand. With their shoes, I had the least chance of irritation. For me that's a must, because if my feet are not OK, not one metre of the run is right. It not only eats into my brain,

but I tend to compensate by running crooked. With this bad posture I get pain in my pelvis and back."

How did your race go?

MARC "The first 80 kilometres ascend to the 3,850-metre high Hope Pass. You then descend completely, then turn around and follow the same route back. My goal was to do the entire circuit in no more than 25 hours. If you succeed, you get something special. In any event, every finisher receives a unique belt buckle with 'Leadville 100' on it. If you are faster than 25 hours, you get an XL version of that buckle. Well, if you make such a long trip, then it seems to me you have to go for it. The first 50 miles I ran in a tight 10 hours. I thought I still had enough margin for the second half, but I found myself battling hard against myself. First again over that mountain pass, while vomiting all the time from altitude

sickness. Just before nightfall, I entered an aid station. There was a young guy who felt like running a little way with me as a *pacer*. This is not so common with us, but in the US, it is. I was alone and could use some support. I did, however, set two conditions: that his gear was in order and that he didn't expect me to talk a lot on the way, because my tongue was already hanging on the floor. At first, his company was very motivating, but in the end he didn't seem to have enough food with him and his headlamp gave out. He had to follow in my footsteps. At a road where I expected that a car would pass by soon, I thanked him for his services. To make matters worse, I lost the signage somewhere in the last 5 kilometres. I did have the route in my sports watch, but the trails in the Rocky Mountains are pitch black at night. Later on, I suddenly saw a parked jeep, which I suspected was from the organization. There was a man sleeping in it. I tapped on the window and the driver woke up. It turned out to be the Leadville race director & co-founder Kenneth Chlouber, whom I'd shaken from his sleep. I'd heard his speech during the briefing before the start. "*You're better than you think you are! You can do more than you think you can do!*" he'd said then. Sounds pretty American, but during the race it was a mantra that gave me a lot of strength. An ultra is a constant game being played out between your ears. Can I do this or can't I? The key is in your head, because after about 100 kilometres there's not much left of your body. I saw Leadville not as a competition, but a mission. That gave me the strength I needed. If you see this idea supported by the words of a hardened ex-miner, who has been marked by life's trails, it gives you focus. I'd not seen anyone for hours and it was mentally heavy going. He got out of his jeep, pointed me in the right direction and said he was convinced I would make it. Right man, right place! Eventually I finished after 24 hours and 57 minutes. I had only 3 minutes left, but it was enough for that XL belt buckle."

Which moment will you never forget?

MARC "Leadville bathes in a culture that is different from the European context. Take the start, for example. Supporters are already there to encourage you. That was strange, especially for a sober Dutchman. I was thinking "what's this all about? We've still got to run this bloody thing, haven't we?" They express their appreciation that you've trained and turn up at the start. The race alone is of course only a short snapshot in such a long journey. Giving up during the race, which more than half of the participants do, is not viewed as failure. Nobody leaves Leadville with a bad feeling. The many volunteers take care of that. And if that doesn't help, you can rinse it out at the country party on the final day. The 'American spirit'!"

A golden tip for future participants?

MARC "Arrive well enough in advance. Leadville is located 3,100 metres up. You need that time to recover from a transatlantic flight and acclimatize to the altitude. I'd never been up to 4,000 metres myself and didn't know exactly what to expect. For

"What? You're crazy! You'll kill someone!" "Well, then we'll be famous, won't we?"

Kenneth Chlouber
LEADVILLE CO-FOUNDER

my acclimatization, I went into the mountains, but after a dozen-metre climb, I was completely off the map. My body was in a nervous overdrive, as if I'd drunk ten mugs of coffee. Very strange to experience that. Eventually I built up slowly. In the week ahead of the race, I climbed several times to 4,000 metres. In itself fantastic, because you're in the middle of the Rocky Mountains. Another reason to get there early enough: the *beer mile* that takes places two days before the race (winks). In addition, I'd also recommend doing the race as part of a crew. And a *pacer* increases your chances of finishing, but first make sure that you're well-matched."

SEX

Timothy is a young man who's also known as Timo. He doesn't get it on asphalt. He prefers running on unpaved paths. Up and down through forests and fields, because flat kilometres have little right to exist in his eyes. Preferably over distances well in excess of those of a classic marathon. He is the hero who initiates me. That's why I don't address him as Timo, but as Mr T. Even without a cool black-painted van, in my eyes he's just as strong as B. A. Baracus of The A-Team.

"If you can run 20 kilometres through Brussels, you can handle 35 kilometres in the Ardennes. And if you can do a 35 km trail, you can also do a 55 km one. Just start more slowly."

Mr T doesn't have a degree in Physical Education. He's an engineer and likes rational reasoning. In his head there is a logical curve that connects the numbers 20, 35 and 55. Without taking into account the injuries that kept me in the stable, the coordinate system in his head shows the trajectory that I completed last year. Why should I doubt myself if he doesn't?

So, a 55 km ultra. Today, in the Walloon-Belgian city of Marche-en-Famenne. The Trail de la Grimace. *What's in a name?*

In Flanders, the notion of 'ultra' calls to mind among the general public the episode that Tom Waes filmed for his programme *Tomtesterom* in 2010. As a layman, he ran the Marathon des Sables in the Moroccan Sahara. According to him, with 252 kilometres over six days, it's one of the toughest multi-day running races in the world. Possibly correct, but then he probably didn't know of the Barkley Marathons. As a programme maker he would immediately have fallen for the concept of this race, because besides being very tough, the race has a very special origin.

DNF

The absurdism starts with the history of this race. In 1977, James Earl Ray, the assassin of Martin Luther King, escaped from a tightly guarded prison in the desolate Frozen Head State Park in Tennessee, USA. Before the arm of the law caught up with him again, in 55 hours he covered just 13 kilometres through the endless forests.

Race director Lazarus 'Laz' Lake reckoned he could certainly have squeezed out 150 kilometres in that time. Or at least as a young boy, before he started chain-smoking and met Mr Beer-Belly. Together with co-founder Karl Henn he marked out a route, christened the child after his former running mate-neighbour Barry Barkley and waited every spring for the mortals who wanted to take their chance in a competition which is somewhere between orienteering and an ultra-trail. The course consists of five rounds of officially 32 kilometres, but in practice 42 kilometres. A total of 16,500 vertical metres climb and descent, or twice up and down Mount Everest - in a maximum of 60 hours. Since 1989, the *where your very best is not good enough* quest has been completed just eighteen times by fifteen people.

The most beautiful failure?

Mr Dan Baglione, then aged 75, covered 3 kilometres of the official circuit, but was on the road for 32 hours.

And the biggest drama?

Garry Robbins in 2017. He was well on his way to becoming the sixteenth finisher of the Barkley. He reached the finish six seconds after the 60-hour cut-off time. But that didn't matter, because he missed the last three kilometres of the official course. Reason enough for a DNF - *Did Not Finish*.

In contrast to the Trail de la Grimace, the Barkley Marathons has no signalling ribbons that indicate the route, nor aid stations where participants can buy food and sports drinks. As proof of their passage, the participants have to tear pages matching their race number out of a dozen hidden books. The titles of the books need no further comment and express the race director's sense of humour. Titles in recent years

"Why should I doubt myself if he doesn't?"

include: *A Time to Die, Southern Discomfort, Up the Down Staircase, Fool, Almost Home, A Week in the Woods, The Idiot, Burnout, Damned, The Human Zoo, Sweet Suffering, Darkness at Noon, The Valley of Death, Body in the Woods, The End, Heart of Darkness, Death Walks the Woods…*

WE'RE OFF!

"Oh yes, Rik… In terms of effort it's a lot harder than 55 kilometres."

"What do you mean?"

"You can count an additional flat kilometre for every hundred vertical metres."

"1,500 vertical metres, that gives an additional 15 kilometres?"

"Yeah!"

"Damn it, Mr T!"

"*Trois, deux, un… Bang! We're off!*"

It's too early for a Sunday. I had to get out of bed before sunrise to be here at the starting line on time. The micro sleep in Mr T's car helped, but I'm not really viable yet.

After a few kilometres through dewy grass, my body gradually comes to life. How might Mr T be doing? Last night he was sitting down to dine at a wedding party, while I, like a monk, had gone to bed on time. In the corner of my eye, I see that he's doing just fine.

At each supply post Mr T, on seeing the foods on display, advises: "Follow my example. I run purely on salt cookies and cola. Sugar, caffeine, carbohydrates and salt. That's all."

I stuff myself every time. Salami and cheese follow each other. And a few nuts. Anything that doesn't taste like those sickly-sweet energy gels which I conscientiously swill down every 45 minutes with water.

At the third supply post my sports watch clocks 42 kilometres. It dawns on me that I've run a marathon for the second time in my life. Frankly, I feel even better than at the start. Where's that 'man with the hammer'?

Again, salt cookies and cola. Salami, cheese and nuts. And paprika crisps, because they didn't have them at the previous supply post.

Still 13 kilometres to go. A piece of cake compared to the already completed marathon. I interrupt the early aperitif and look at Mr T. On his face I notice that last night's wedding feast is wreaking its vengeance.

"You can't achieve something if there is no chance of failure," says Lazarus Lake.

Would I dare? Accelerate and see if I can outrun my teacher today? I strategically keep quiet for a few more kilometres, but plug in the earphones of my mp3 player. On the menu the title track of the first CD that I bought as a thirteen-year-old:

Roots, bloody roots
I believe in our fate

We don't need to fake
It's all we wanna be
Watch me freak.

Together with Sepultura chief Max Cavalera I unleash my devils. Mr T clings on a little longer, but then lets me go. Three songs later, for a long climb, I fish my collapsible running sticks from my running backpack to force me up. A grin, because soon I will belong to the club that can scornfully say "You ran a marathon? So cute!"

Another 7 kilometres to the finish.

The descent is a lot more technical than the previous climbs and descents. I have to look carefully where I place my feet and running sticks. On a slightly too high rock it all goes wrong. My left running stick breaks in half and I fall forward. I slide over the rock with my right knee and lie still a few seconds before I check if I've broken anything. Crestfallen I fold up my sticks.

PRIDE COMES BEFORE A FALL?

I carefully continue the descent. When not much later Mr T appears from round the corner, I realize that my parricide has failed. In the 10 seconds that he will need to get to me, a hammer, a baseball bat and a crowbar all hit me at once.

"Everything OK, Rik?"
  "*Neje!*" I shout, ashamed.
  "Come, it's only 6 kilometres!" Mr T says paternally.

I feel like a peeled onion. Without realizing it, I'm flayed to my core. Everyday worries and annoyances no longer exist. My ego is dissolved in lactic acid. This zone, where Mr T seems to be at home, is new to me. Everything hurts.

HOW DO I DEAL WITH THIS?

Jason Robillard, author of the unorthodox trail handbook *Never wipe your ass with a squirrel*, is categorical: 'Sex!'

His trick is to associate pain with something pleasant, just as a sadomasochist associates a painful fetish with an orgasm. He describes the praxis as a solid example of conditioning, in which you couple a neutral stimulus with the pleasure of orgasm. If you then apply this neutral stimulus to kill the pain in such conditions, the pain eventually becomes something you enjoy.

I feel like a zombie. My thinking is slow. Sex is the last thing I'm thinking of. After a few minutes in Mr T's wake, I sign to him that he has no need to wait for me. We walk a bit and I want more of that. He shuffles off with small steps. Not much later the tears roll down my cheeks, but I have no idea why. I rub my eyes dry and try to keep the pace.

The corn along the field track sways gently to and fro. The hundreds of views and impressions I've reviewed over the past 6 hours and 45 minutes have beaten me to a pulp. I didn't know Belgium could be so pristine and wild.

I'm present.

In the distance I hear the commentator's rattle at the finish. I squeeze the last drops of water from my drinking bottle and begin to jog again. A few minutes later I run over the finishing line.

If you want to run, run a mile.
If you want to experience a different life,
run a marathon.
If you want to talk to God, run an ultra.

Dixit Dean Karnazes, author of *Ultramarathon Man: Confessions of an All-Night Runner.*

Clubmate Johan proudly presents me with a glass of local beer.

My pupils are wide open.

Actually, an ultra is a long controlled foreplay about which you say afterwards: "Tiens, I came four times on the way!" ▲▲▲

Spain
ZEGAMA-
AIZKORRI

Where the fuck's my shoe?!

Zegama
ZEGAMA-AIZKORRI MENDI MARATOIA

42KM | 26MI • D+ 2,750M | 9,022FT

- ⊕ FIESTA!
- ⊕ Fiery supporters
- ⊕ Small participants' field

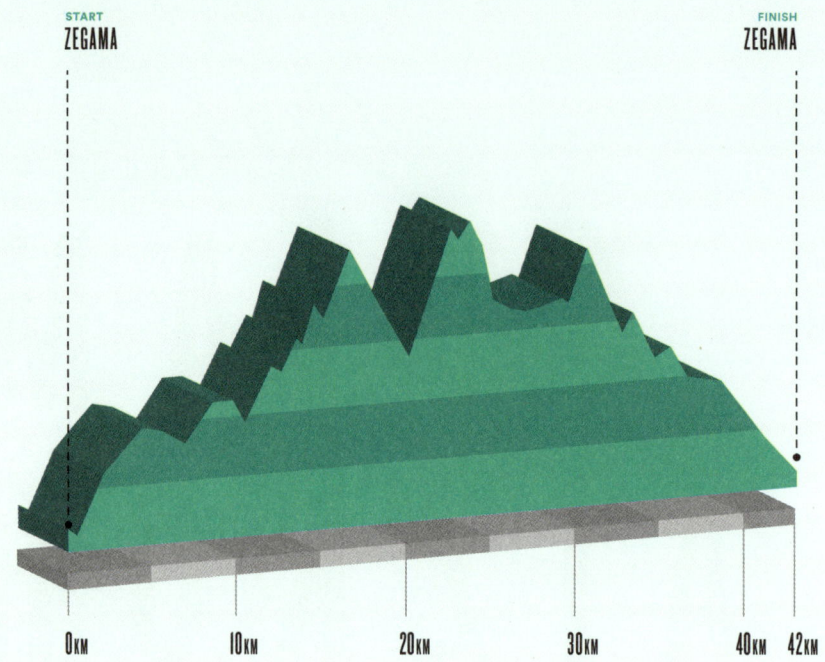

START
ZEGAMA

FINISH
ZEGAMA

0KM   10KM   20KM   30KM   40KM 42KM

OTHER DISTANCES
ZEGAMA-AIZKORRI KILOMETRO VERTICAL
5,2KM | 3MI • D+ 1,015M | 3,330FT

EDUARD SERRANO

Age 36 • Computer engineer
Barcelona • Spain

Why did you choose this race?

EDUARD "I started running in around 2010. Before that, I did quite a lot of sport, but that didn't include running. Rather skiing, rock climbing and mountaineering. For me, the mountains were already familiar terrain, but not for running. At that time, I occasionally worked as a hut guard in the Pyrenees. At one point, a trail runner came along. A real *gear junkie*, with a much too large sports watch. I was immediately bitten! I wanted to do that too! I started like everyone else with 5 kilometres. After this, I built up to 10 kilometres. And from 10 kilometres to 20 kilometres, and from there to the Barcelona marathon. I'm skinny by build, so running suits me well. That guy with his oversized sports watch became a friend, with whom I ended up running my first ultra. After that, it dawned on me that I wasn't made for the super long work. Running through nights without sleep? No thanks. My mate then signed up for Zegama. Me too. He had already registered every year, but had never been selected. You can already guess what happened. He didn't get a starting number again and I was lucky first time (laughs). I immediately said that I'd do it. I'm Catalan. Probably I don't need to tell you that, as such, I'm inclined to the Basque cause. A race in the Basque mountains was right up my street. The small field also appealed to me, but it was mainly the circus, with the thousands of supporters, that made my mouth water and motivated me to prepare well. Where else in the world do you have a running race in the mountains where spectators shout you on so hard? It's just like a mountain pass on the Tour de France, full of fiery supporters."

How did you prepare?

EDUARD "I intended to enjoy it, without being too hard on myself. During the week, I did three times a winding 12-kilometre tour. On weekends, I went to the Pyrenees for extra denivelation. I was keen to sharpen my condition as much as possible. The terrain as such wasn't a concern, even though the course is sometimes quite technical. I had the advantage that my father had taken me into the mountains since I was a child. Together with my climbing experience, you can say that the mountains are my natural habitat."

How did your race go?

EDUARD "I assumed it was going to rain on the race day. Basque country, you know (winks). That prediction was correct, which of course means extra mud. This makes the race

Race secret

Zegama-Aizkorri was created by locals to combat rural flight and put the mountain village on the map. With processions, the village already had a solid tradition of feasts next to little chapels high in the mountains. Cheese, tortilla, ham and wine in the backpack and up you go! The wild scenes on the flanks of the massif don't happen out of the blue. Anyone thinking that the participants will miss the dance is mistaken. The after-party following the race seems to be legendary. If you want to drink something, don't run too fast. It's a public secret that the last participant passing through the last aid station receives a big bottle of Rioja. Alcohol is sugars, and sugar is fuel. Cheers!

even harder going than it already is. It was a fast start. This has everything to do with the cut-off time around kilometre seven. I understand why, for safety reasons, the organization wants to avoid as much as possible having participants strung out too far apart on the mountain. Anyway, I made the cut-off time and could take it a little easier on the first climb to Aratz. After the San Adrian tunnel, the climb to Aizkorri began. The route there was rows thick with supporters. Unbelievable how they shout you on. Because there are only 450 participants, viewers quickly find your starting number in the competition brochure. As you plough your way uphill, all the time it's *"Venga, Eduard de Barcelona, venga!"* And also constantly *"Oso ondo!"*

which in Basque means 'Come on! Very good!' A madhouse, I swear. After Aitxuri, you dive down the other side, and then in a wide bow you climb again along the fourth and last summit over the massif. After that, it's 12 kilometres downhill to the finish. I really had goosebumps when I arrived. My wife was also waiting for me. It was fantastic. Afterwards, so many people asked how it had gone, just because they saw from my chest number that I was a participant. I'd never experienced that in any other race. I'd planned to enjoy it as much as possible. That was the objective. On the way, I fell a few times, but that's part of it. I was constantly smiling. That helps. Positive vibes are just as important and significant to me in a race as a good condition."

Which moment will you never forget?

EDUARD "With the rain, the descent to Zegama was very muddy. Many people lost their shoes, which were sucked into the mud. It happened to me too. I'd calculated it in my head - I'm a computer engineer, and as such am used to numbers and statistics. Average speed, distance, number of vertical metres... I had a chance to complete the race within 6 hours and 30 minutes. But suddenly it hit me too. I got stuck in the mud and lost one of my shoes. There you are in the middle of a forest: "*Where the fuck*'s my shoe?!" Now I can laugh at that, but at that moment it was a little bit of war."

A golden tip for future participants?

EDUARD "It's 42 kilometres, but it's not a flat marathon. Make sure you've trained adequately. A full 2,700 metres of vertical climbing is no cakewalk. It would also be a sin to consume a race like Zegama without proper conditioning. This race is a grand cru, to be enjoyed. Also, bring a good windproof and waterproof jacket, because a T-shirt really is insufficient. It can be pretty cold high in the mountains!"

"It's not artificial. It's something pure. It comes from the inside."

Dimitris Theodorakakos

POOP

At the entrance to the restaurant is a wheelchair with the petrol station's logo. I hesitate. Most of my running club companions have been standing for a long time at the soup kitchen buffet. I'm barely halfway through the revolving door. I'm broken but not paralysed. Can I make it?

"You don't mean that, Rik!"
  "Well, it can't be otherwise."

I collapse into the leather of the wheelchair. I glide over the wheels with my hands and rediscover the importance of suppleness. The past few hours were sedentary in the car. I had to figure myself out after sitting still for so long. I've never been so stiff. I'm like setting concrete.

With tray on lap I roll from the cold to the hot buffet. My clubmates watch the scene giggling. My own fault, but I don't regret my first ever mountain marathon, which I'm just back from, even though it was a chronicle of a pre-announced death.

How did the scenario go?

Well, you get back on your feet with runners' knee and heel track. Half a year to become a runner again. Long distances broken with intensive spurts. And as often as possible into the Ardennes for vertical climb. To be able to trot again you have to go through the desert, but too much turned out to be too much. My shins were on fire. The doctor prescribed me five weeks without running to avoid stress fractures. Precisely the last five weeks before the start of that exotic Marathon du Mont-Blanc.

A man would swear blue murder for less.

The plan to swim and cycle as an alternative training remained a plan, because those sports mean nothing to me. Compared with them, propping up the bar with friends and colleagues was often a more obvious choice.

NIGHT OWL, YES

Salvation in places of destruction!
  Perhaps these shins were in the first place a signal that there are also non-runners in this society. And that among those

non-runners are also very good friends and family, who also deserve time and attention.

Only a week ago did I don my running shoes once again. A 10 km local race as a test. The bodywork still cracked, but didn't disintegrate. I wisely decided not to return to the sports doctor. Or at least not before the marathon. Sometimes it's better to be creative with doctors' advice.

Yesterday it was very hot. The race day itself is bathed in drizzle. Is this the high day we were looking forward to for so long? We 1,500 runners take up position in the square in front of the iconic church. I know the sanctuary from YouTube. The images of a panting Kilian Jornet are still fresh in my memory.

Chamonix church - Mont Blanc summit - Chamonix church in 4 hours 57 minutes and 40 seconds.

The 23-year-old record in tatters, broken by 14 minutes. I remember how in the accompanying interview the Catalan always pronounced Mont Blanc like *Mont Blank*. Like a cute little hill in his own Pyrenees. This Ferrari of mountain runners stands at the front among his kind. He won here the past two years. Will he pull it off again today?

'*Dix, neuf, huit...*'
  Legs, let's talk... Shins, be careful!
  You too, Mr Beer-Belly. No fancy stuff, buddy!

42 kilometres, D+ 2,136 metres and D- 1,700 metres.
  It's just a long walk. Probably a fast long walk, but you've been able to rest up enough now. Today we'll be a trail runner again.
  Shall we agree on that?

"*Deux, un! Départ du douzième Marathon du Mont-Blanc!*"

The pack pushes foot by foot over the starting line and gradually moves into a gallop. Despite the miserable weather, we run through a double row of supporters with tinkling cowbells.

ASSEZ ROULANT

Again Kilian's words blow through my mind. In a preview of the race he judged the first 20 kilometres as *assez roulant* - a bit up and down. It sounds arrogant to cut a mountain marathon in two, but he's more than right. We simply curl to the end of the valley, remaining all the time under the tree line. *Assez roulant* is hard work for an under-trained mortal.

"Sometimes it's better to be creative with doctors' advice."

UNGRATEFUL FUCKING SPORT

'If it gets too hard, just slow down.'

The reassuring adage of the Swedish icon Emelie Forsberg, Kilian Jornet's sweetheart, jumps to mind. Walking at 3 kilometres an hour, although slower than running, is still faster than standing still at 0 kilometres an hour.

The number of raindrops is not reducing either. And the temperature also drops with the altitude. Just before l'Aiguillette des Posettes the wind becomes more severe. I stop and take gloves from my running back-pack. The granite ridge itself was taken out of the course by the race director this morning as being too dangerous. Then directly to Le Tour. No disaster, because with the fog the view of the Mont Blanc massif is nothing to write home about.

Ungrateful fucking sport.

From steady plodding I change to running with gravity as an ultimate pep pill.

Earphones in. Play. Dancing! Dancing!

The elongated descent on wide gravel roads is a rave party of three songs. Delicious running! I check my watch in the valley. 26.9 kilometres in 3 hours and 23 minutes. Afterwards I will learn that Kilian Jornet reached the finish in Chamonix almost simultaneously.

How does that guy do that?

I have to get started again. Honestly, I let myself go a bit during the descent and now pay the price. My legs feel like porridge.

I'm not quite halfway, but my legs are already beginning to go numb. The rain-soaked path is ploughed and slippery.

I don't dare to admit it at the aid station, but it's not been that simple. I chose to take part in this race because I absolutely wanted the experience. The way I complete it is secondary. After another glass of cola, the trail meanders up the mountain flank towards Switzerland. From 1,260 metres to 1,997 metres. I've never done such a long climb. Yes, with a trekking backpack and mountain boots, but not in sports shoes and against the clock.

The path fans up in narrow hairpin bends and the large number of runners forces you to take it at walking pace.

Traffic jam when climbing a mountain: happiness in an accident.

Learning the hard way, with just 15 kilometres to go. I take my fourth energy gel of the day. Come on, this should work!

A few kilometres later, the trail seeks the other side of the valley. Another 400 metres up and then double down to Chamonix. A few more hours of feeling like a chicken in a Flemish waterzooi – spiced with rhododendron and juniper berry picked in the valley here.

EMERGENCY SITUATION

"Hey ho! Attention! Qu'est-ce que tu fais?!"

I no longer answer. I'm already 3 metres below. My intestines are screaming blue murder. Those damn energy gels! I squat down on the steep mountainside and try to wriggle out of my trousers before fouling myself.

"Ça va là-bas? Tu es tombé?"
   "Non, non!" I will hurry as quickly as possible. *"Je suis euh... aux toilettes!"*

To make things even worse, I can't get out of my new running pants. Knotted them too tight this morning. Stay calm, ignore the cramps and potter about. Just in time I manage to disentangle everything.

Relief and a pine cone as toilet paper.

As long as toilet paper is not on the list of compulsory equipment for a race, the nonchalant human being must, in acute emergency situations, use what is at hand.

I climb to my feet and crawl back to the path on all fours. Back into the race. I hobble a bit, because the spring is broken. At the last aid station, I sit with a coke staring into nowhere. As if drinking at the bar with the 'man with the hammer' himself. I decide to become a real trail runner again as soon as possible.

A privilege, with corresponding duties.

The joints creak horribly on the last descent. No, no more dance steps this time. My thighs still work as stabilizers but no longer as shock absorbers, which means that my lower back is taking it. I feel like a crooked old man trying to get his bus.

Asphalt finally appears again, and with it supporters.

"Allez, les gars! Vous êtes presque là!"

I turn into the Rue Joseph Vallot. The rows behind the crowd control barriers become denser. The cheering and applause louder. I come back to life.

"Bravo! Encore 300 mètres!"

I see the arrival arch around the bend. A pro forma final sprint. I jump over the finishing line. My second marathon is a fact - even though I've run in anything but proper race pace.

Congratulations from the club members.

"I really had to poop just now!" I throw out as a thank you. After 7 hours and 8 minutes of slogging through the mountains, you no longer think about protocol.

Fortunately, we speak the same language.
▲▲▲

USA
WESTERN STATES 100-MILE ENDURANCE RUN

159.4 km | 100 mi • D+ 7,170 m | 23,524 ft

*"I'm doing this...
I'm running Western
States... I'M REALLY
RUNNING WESTERN
STATES!!!!
And now I'm walking
Western States."*

Jeffery Lung
WWW.THERUNFACTORY.COM

JUNGLE

Despite the fresh morning, the leather of the back seat clings sweatily to my half-bare buttocks. Do I still have a fever? Instinctively I feel my forehead. I ask myself if I wouldn't have done better to stay in bed. I chase away the thought. *It's better to burn out than to fade away*, the late Kurt Cobain wrote - a helping thought in this context, even if the quote's originally from Neil Young. After two days of soaking wet fever dreams, I couldn't care a heck how I'll feel later. Four walls - interspersed only with high-speed visits to the smallest room - are still just four walls.

Mr Beer-Belly, you look a little pale. Are you OK?

My driver's thinking. Left or right here? The piece of paper I gave him with the destination hangs like a cigarette between his lips. With two hands he gives the steering wheel a quarter turn. Left is about the same direction as right. Sounds illogical, but what is straight back in Belgium is crooked here. Buddha provides, they say, although Buddha did a dirty trick on me with that

gigantic mojito with far too much crushed ice. The Enlightened One clearly doesn't live here in the tap water.

We stop again. My driver winds down his window and picks up my note from between his rotten teeth. Incomprehensible chatter. Hands point the way to my destination like nervous snakes. My race starts in half an hour.

COME ON! DRIVE, MAN!

I take a sip of my water bag and carefully rub the bump on my tibia. Sensitive, but not painful. Clearly different from half a year ago, when I'd jump up several metres into the air at the slightest touch. The injury that halted me after the Mont Blanc Marathon was a stress fracture on my right shin. Too much impact stress in too short a build-up period, with that mountain marathon in Chamonix acting as a Japanese kamikaze pilot scoring a direct hit.

Jusshi Reisho! / Sacrifice your ~~life~~ leg!'

Today I'm making my comeback. An 18-kilometre race. These are also my first training kilometres. Incautious, except that that I made a pain-free trek during the last three weeks. My calves are back tight again.

The circuit first leads participants 700 metres upwards over 4 kilometres to the summit of Jamacho. The remaining 14 kilometres are a descent along a narrow path through untouched jungle.

He who can walk, can run. This has to succeed.

Slowly the stalls and concrete houses of Kathmandu make way for green and steep hills. My taxi seems to be approaching my final destination. A hypothesis I see confirmed in a young woman in running kit who is charging uphill in front of us.

I sign the driver to stop and wind down my window.

"Do you go to the Jamacho Jungle Run? Do you need a ride?"

She seems a little lost, but then shrugs her shoulders and gets in. Now it's my turn for a surprise. Isn't this Mira Rai, Nepal's top mountain runner? I doubt, but eventually take the plunge. With thanks to the University of Social Media:

"Weren't you second after Stevie Kramer in that 50K-race in Hong Kong last year?"

Her eyes light up. A big smile.
   Yes.

Mira's not a kitten to handle without gloves. She has no claws, but a Chinese Type 67

machine gun on a tripod. Or rather past tense, had, because that civil war between the Maoists and the Nepalese government ended in 2006. How did she get caught up in all that? Mira's heimat lies in the poverty-stricken countryside, where adult women belong in the home. For a while, exempted from this before marriage, Mira worked as a porter. Fetching water for her family and carrying loads over the mountains for a fee. Until the rising Maoists did their rounds, preaching their worldview of equality. Bacon for Mira's adventurous mouth. She ran away from home and, like tens of thousands of her peers, followed a training course with the Maoists. She didn't set foot on the battlefield, but underwent a Spartan training in the jungle full of constant denivelations. After the civil war the genie was out of the bottle. She went to Kathmandu and accidentally landed in an ultra, which she won in her category – in fact, she was the only woman. She had no specific running equipment, competition knowledge or energy gels. She simply saw a chance and grabbed it with two hands. The rest of her story is history, embraced by her sponsor Salomon.

Does she still keep that whopper of a machine gun in her training bag?

"*You run?*" she asks in broken English.

I nod - with a wobbly head, as usual in this subcontinent. I let slip that it's my first race since a long injury. I'm a running version of the Tibetan Book of the Dead. Every time die and be born again. Or does that sound too dramatic? I pulse with Mira.

"*Haha! Good, good! You run again, good. After race, come say hello!*"

We get out of the taxi in Balaju. A tangle of all kinds of runners: Nepalese mountain guides wanting to keep their physical form while waiting for customers, deadly serious Western trail runners, Nepalese *weekend warriors* with laptop fingers and giggling schoolgirls in slippers. I'm not sure in which category I belong, but the start number ensures unity.

Race director Richard Bull jumps onto a table: "*Good morning! Please proceed to the starting line. We're about to race!*"

With 87 runners we shuffle to Phulbari Gate - the military checkpoint at the entrance to the nature park. Richard improvises with his heel a starting line in the gravel, behind which we all take up position. He performs the entire manoeuvre with a bright red inflated balloon between his elbow and torso.

"*Ten, nine, eight…*"

The balloon goes up - sandwiched between Richard's fingernails.

"*Three, two, one… BANG!*"

The red balloon is no more. The pack flies up the steps. 700 metres uphill over 4 kilometres. Like Beatrix's initiation test in the Kill Bill movie. On starting her apprenticeship with Chinese kung fu master Pai Mei, she's given the task of fetching water in the valley and carrying the buckets up the steep stairs to the temple.

I check the altitude on my sports watch. Almost halfway. I can't do it running. It's really too steep for me. Honestly? I'm out of breath. Two days of fever and tourist diarrhoea have wrung me dry, and for this kind of bodywork, you'd best have fluid reserves in your cells. One step too many and I stop. Suddenly my head starts to spin.

PANIC

"Rik, stay calm, it's not as bad as the previous two times on this trip", I mutter to myself. "At the 5,416 metre high Thorung La you were overcome by the thin air and you panicked in the vast snowy landscape with not a soul in sight. You even shouted for help for the first time in your life. But it worked out OK, the bad feeling passed. And in Kyanjin Gompa you were helped at 3,860 metres as a solo trekker with rising altitude sickness by a local angel who carried your backpack several hundred metres lower. Buddha provided. Then too it passed. Now you are just a little sick. Get a hold of yourself!"

I decide to walk up to the top. Pushing today doesn't make sense. I look back and search for companionship. A few hairpin turns lower are two other participants. I wait for them.

"*Hi, I'm Rik. Mero name Rik ho*", I try semi-bilingually.
  "*Namaste! My name is Ang Gumbu Sherpa.*"
  "*And I'm Norsang Sherpa.*"

Damn, I have two *Sherpas* next to me...

Isn't their genetic advantage blood doping? I rub it laconically under their noses. Laughter, and each takes a selfie with that strange Belgian. Together we complete the second half of the climb. On the way, they ask me about my experiences in their country - interrupted by regular breaks for landscape snaps and selfies.

The viewing platform on the top is full of Tibetan prayer flags. The red-green-blue-yellow vibrates in the bright morning light. I drop out of breath with my sherpas onto the railing. In the geographic basin below us lies Kathmandu under a thick layer of smog with an azure blue sky above it. More photos. This time I participate.

The sherpas start the descent with a whoop. I chew a bit more on a muesli bar and take a few gulps of water, which cuts my breath.

"OK, Rik … This is your test. It's now 14 kilometres downhill. Think about your shins! Let gravity do its job: don't fall, but slide," my inner coach instructs me.

With short steps I jump from stone to stone and in the curves like skiers look for higher terrain to brake my speed. With my arms, I try to keep my balance.

After 3 kilometres I make a first evaluation of my former stress fracture. It seems the pain's staying away. My hikes with thousands of metres of denivelation have laid a foundation in which my body knows what to do. Muscles have a memory, bones and tendons unfortunately do not. In their ignorance, they are present today - until further notice, at least.

Endorphins, I love you.

My sherpas stop again. Again snapshots with crazy faces. I sigh. I feel much better than when going uphill and am fed up with their dawdling. Noisy chatting and photos can also be done after the race. This is and will remain a race.

I go to the head and force them to fall into single file. Protests and whistling from behind my back are the result, but I don't care. I have wings again and can fly again. I turn on my mp3 player. Moby is on my shoulders during the flight and whispers in my ears.

You might run on for a long time
Run on, ducking and dodging
Run on, children, for a long time
Let me tell you God Almighty gonna cut you down

A few minutes later I dive under yet another branch and I look briefly behind.

No one.

Have I just shaken off those sherpas? The attendant euphoria is short-lived. Another participant emerges from behind the curvature of the hill. He runs towards me. This isn't right. Who's running in the wrong direction here: he or I? He points to the path in front of me and makes a cross with his two arms. I pluck the earphones from my ears. I'd not noticed until then that the vegetation around the narrow path had become denser. The organization was already mean with their security tape signalling, but I was too deeply absorbed in my music to notice its total absence.

LOST IN THE NEPALESE JUNGLE

Well done, Rik Merchie. Do you never learn?

I retrace my steps with my route companion. Looking for signalling tapes and, failing that, footprints and flattened vegetation. After fifteen minutes of track searching, a signal tape brings redemption. We squat down and determine the running direction on the basis of dozens of footprints.

Together we scurry away again. A quarter of an hour later, applause follows at the finishing line from sherpas and a thumbs-up from race director Richard. Mira too notices me. She's squatting around a self-lit fire with some companions and beckons me over.

"Good? No pain?"
  "No, all fine! And you? Did you win?"
  "Not win, but first female!"

Obviously first woman. And eleventh in the overall ranking. I took an hour longer than she did, but I don't care. I rub my shin and just feel sweat and dust. Being able to run again after a long injury is like waking up and realizing your fever dream is over. ▲▲▲

"Endorphins,
I love you."

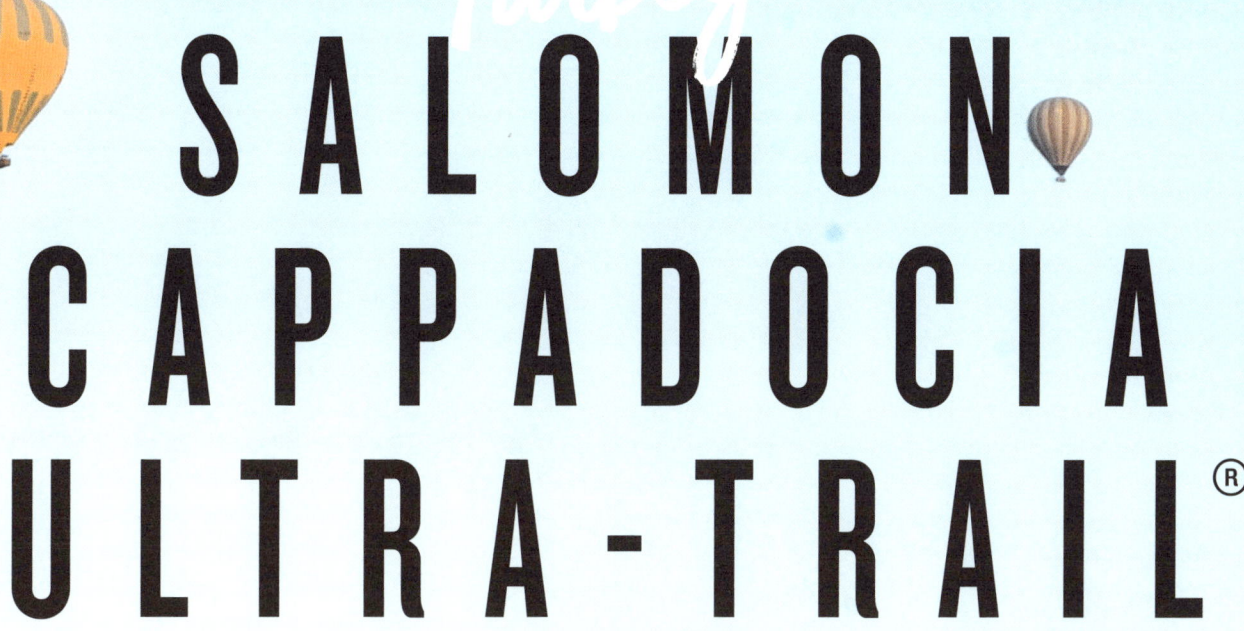

Turkey

SALOMON CAPPADOCIA ULTRA-TRAIL®

It doesn't have to be the Alps every time.

Turkey

SALOMON CAPPADOCIA ULTRA-TRAIL®

119KM | 70.8MI
D+ 3,730M | 12,238FT

- Beyond the clichés
- Friendly & exotic
- Value for money

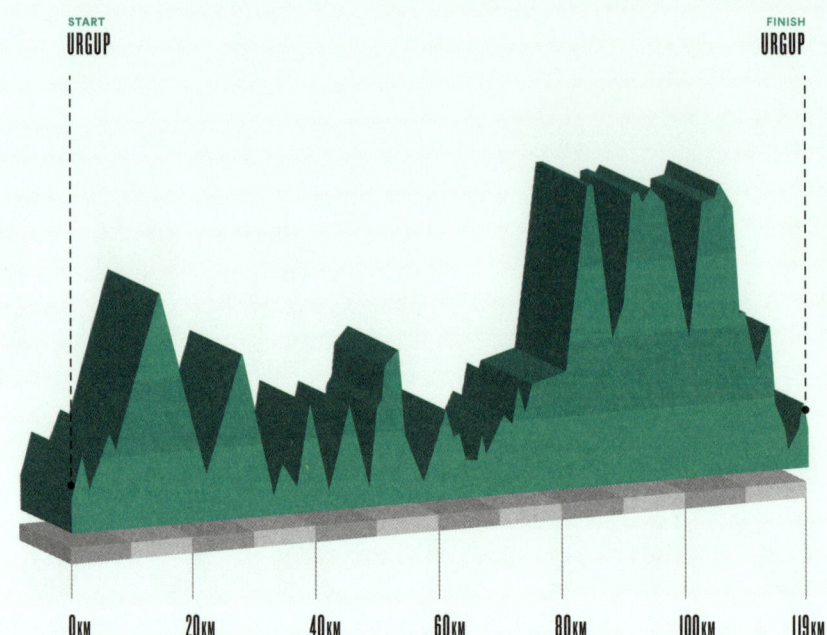

START
URGUP

FINISH
URGUP

0KM   20KM   40KM   60KM   80KM   100KM   119KM

OTHER DISTANCES

CAPPADOCIA SHORT TRAIL
38KM | 23.6MI • D+ 1,120M | 3,674FT

CAPPADOCIA MEDIUM TRAIL
63KM | 39.1MI • D+ 2,030M | 6,660FT

MARTIN VEREECKEN

Age 46 • IT consultant
Ghent • Belgium

Why did you choose this race?

MARTIN "It wasn't me who chose this 114 km race, but my girlfriend (laughs). It was a surprise for my birthday. That's to say, it was intended as a surprise, but it turned out differently. I'd already received a text message from Christof, a running mate, on my birthday. He had also registered and had seen my name on the participants' list. I guessed that this had something to do with my birthday, and I suspected that my girlfriend was behind it. I pretended as best I could that I was surprised when she gave it to me as a gift, but Christof was a legendary telltale. But yes, it was a good present. As an IT professional, I spend a lot of time in my head and in front of a screen. Trail running is my way of connecting with my body. So this gift was not a poisoned one. Especially when I got to see some pictures and photos of the race. Cappadocia is a unique environment. Mountainous, but not your typical Swiss mountain landscape with snowy peaks. Those rock dwellings that you find here and there looked fantastic to me. Yes, it made sense, but not as a purely physical challenge. I've already run the UTMB® twice. Each time I trained for it in a very focused way. For both editions, I gave all I could in order to achieve a result that I could be proud of. I'd decided in advance that I would not be so hard on myself on this trail. Here in Belgium, you find similar challenges in terms of denivelation metres. So the plan was not to run myself into the ground but to enjoy it."

How did you prepare?

MARTIN "It didn't go that well. Because I wasn't running for a result, I hadn't approached it so systematically. Moreover, I was injured three months before Cappadocia. That came from being a bit too enthusiastic with my Vibram Fivefingers. That's footwear for barefoot running, as in the book *Born to Run*. I went on a trail running race with them in the Belgian Ardennes. The path was strewn in many places with jagged rocks and one of my heels couldn't take that very well, and damaged the fat pads that protect the heel bone against impact stress. Luckily, I had my regular shoes in my running backpack so that I could change on the way. But the damage had already been done. Eventually I also got an inflammation on the Achilles tendon on my other leg. I had run crookedly to compensate for the pain in my heel. Probably it was this that brought on this second injury. I was forced to reduce training kilometres and had to drop out of the Ultra Tour Monte Rosa. As a test, I ran a 30-kilometre race a week before the Cappadocia. As I set off for Turkey, I had few expectations on the athletic level."

How did your race go?

MARTIN "The course has two loops. The first is 60 kilometres long and forms the second shortest variant of the event. I'd planned to run the full race if I didn't feel any abnormal aches after that first loop. Given my limited training volume, I knew it could be heavier than usual. That's why I was happy to start with a running mate. We had agreed to stay together. He had run the TDS in Chamonix a few months before. He was still recovering from this, but he had to and was determined to do this race to gather enough points to register for the UTMB®. He was therefore not 100% either. When around the 30th kilometre he admitted that he was finding it quite hard going, I was secretly relieved. After all, Christof is a good runner, who has already run the Grand Trail des Templiers in addition to the TDS. OK, shared suffering tastes sweeter. His descents were faster, while I climbed better. So we pulled together. The course itself was very beautiful. Especially in that first loop, there were many gorges and rock houses. The second loop was less satisfying. With wide, sandy paths, it was at times dull and boring. But in the end, my injuries didn't give me too much trouble. Also fitness-wise, I succeeded better than I had hoped. Where I had a hard time in the middle part, for Christof the last 10 kilometres were especially heavy. The final kilometres we walked more than we ran. Christof was not up to smiling for a nice finish photo, but we made it."

Which moment will you never forget?

MARTIN "The spaghetti and the bean bags at the *aid station*! No, seriously... As a Western European, you are running in what is clearly a different culture. Everywhere you see the logos of the famous trail running brands, of course, but to see a woman signaller with headscarf, wide dress and long coat and then a Salomon shirt on top takes some getting used to. Call it trail running beyond the cliché of classic Western mountain massifs. For me, that's an added asset which makes it worth considering this race. I would also mention that, with a 70 euros registration fee, this race is quite cheap compared to other ultras. You also get value for that money: an extensive goodie bag, a substantial discount on tourist activities and transport to and from the airport."

A golden tip for future participants?

MARTIN "If you participate, opt for 60 kilometres or 30 kilometres. Unless the second loop of the 114 km course changes in the future, you don't have to run yourself into the ground to experience Cappadocia. If you do opt for the longest race, make sure you have a running buddy or pick up someone on the way in order to get through the night. I don't mean that sexually. 54 kilometres is really long if the course doesn't surprise you or really challenge you."

"You're not afraid, you're not afraid. Do not be afraid. You will not be afraid."

Bethany Turley
FINISHER 2016 SALOMON CAPPADOCIA ULTRA-TRAIL®

MILESTONE

With twelve participants, all virgins for this type of race, we are tripping on the starting line. I take it all too seriously, but for once I estimate my chances of winning as good. I will sell my skin dearly. A few seconds before the start. I push the earphones of my mp3 player deeper and press play.

Two great European narcotics
Alcohol and Christianity
I know which one I prefer.

Mike Skinner's parlando seemed a good harbinger for the coming storm. Three cans of beer stand in front of my feet. A fourth is in my hand. The task is simple. A *beer mile*: 4 x 400 metres, interrupted only by a beer drunk to the dregs. Vomiting costs you an extra round. The current world record is 4 minutes and 34 seconds. Idiotic and student-like, but justified in the context. It's the *Gentse Feesten*, the annual Ghent festival, when my home city bathes for ten days in alcohol, puke and semen.

What are a few beers then?

I stand next to my main competitor - a football fan and thus logically an experienced beer drinker. He's not lost training sessions from a running injury. With pure running, I'll beat him today, I think. What combining this with carbonated beer will be like remains a mystery to me.

The starting shot.

Come on, Mr Beer-Belly!
 You know this shit!

I rip open my first can of beer, tilt my head into my neck and breathe deep one last time. The first ten gulps go down well. Gulp eleven meets with resistance and I notice how my main competitor is turning his can ostentatiously over his head. Before I realize it, he passes the first corner of the athletics track.

Jesus Christ, to swill like that!

BORN TO BOOZE?

The last gulp. I pitch my empty can onto the grass and set off in pursuit. Fast, but not too fast. The prizes are handed out at the finishing line, and we're not there yet. Belching loudly, I pass the second corner. With the air out of my system, I speed up. Slowly but surely I creep up on my main competitor. At the fourth corner I'm right behind him. Let him do the work, I think to myself, in the last round I finish him off.

Simultaneously we open our second can. I take a few seconds to recover from my overtaking manoeuvre. By the time I've taken my first gulp, my main competitor is already out of the starting blocks.

Where did he learn to drink like that?

Sports and alcohol are *prima facie* fire and water. A Miami sociology professor once threw these two parameters into a statistical survey of 200,000 adult compatriots. What turned out? Moderate to heavy drinkers did sport more often and longer than light drinkers and total abstainers. Aware of the accumulated surplus of calories, movement serves as a remedy to stay healthy - whether or not out of inherent guilt. If alcohol can be a catalyst for movement, then perhaps it's not so devilish after all?

In addition, a reverse reasoning also exists. A physicist from Texas points out that athletes with a preference for beatifying endorphins tend to also have a weakness for the anaesthetic effect of alcohol.

Is that why I wanted to go through with this?

A beer mile combines the best of two worlds, but is not the limit of the spectrum. For example, since 2017 there has been in Wales a *beer ultra* with 50 kilometres and eleven cans of beer. In addition, there are lots of drinking clubs with a running problem in the Anglo-Saxon world. A collective pub crawl aka *hashing* in running shoes, with fast runners doing some extra loops to wait for the slower ones to catch up. Maybe not that crazy? Bar counter-proppers get into movement and obsessive runners learn a lesson in socialization. Last but not least: beer works well as a recovery drink. The polyphenols present in it are natural antioxidants and prevent inflammation. Unfortunately, they are as present in alcohol-free beer as in beer with alcohol, but no one needs to know that.

The second round is a repetition of the first. I catch up with my main competitor and try to dose my pace. At the line we simultaneously open the third can. I have to catch my breath again before I can drink. My main competitor has already left at my first gulp. Although my stomach pinches, I still try to maintain a strong drinking rate. Behind me my coach starts his third can. I realize that I must continue. I wring the can empty and start again. First quietly jogging and belching as much as possible to get all that carbon dioxide out of my stomach, and only speeding up.

When I again close in on my main competitor, I decide to bet on my fourth and final round. He will crack.

Mr Beer-Belly! Mr Beer-Belly! Mr Beer-Belly!

TIME FOR A #TAG MR BEER-BELLY?

It doesn't surprise me that long-distance runners can drink solidly. The two disciplines intertwine more than one might think. Excessive drinking and ultras can both lead to vomiting, urinating in public and serious injuries. Both demand considerable training to cultivate tolerance. And afterwards, with stiff legs after a heavy ultra or with a hangover after a wild night, you swear you'll never do anything like that again. Only to admit a weekend later that you've registered for another race or are drunk again on that nocturnal dance floor.

Beer number four.

My stomach is blocking, but now it has to happen. All or nothing. I ignore the belching and set off in pursuit. A handful of spectators are screaming at the finish.

Half a round to go.

I approach, but run totally out of breath. I cross the finishing line seven seconds after my main competitor. I acknowledge his superiority. We both take a can of beer to celebrate the end of the race.

I've been waiting 32 years, but I finally have a podium place in running. The flush of the victory and the high endorphins were already there, but now the alcohol is also kicking in.

Four cans in 7 minutes and 3 seconds.

#silver

A round of applause for Mr Beer-Belly! ▲▲▲

New Zealand
TARAWERA ULTRA MARATHON

I felt like a
world-famous
rock star

Rotorua

TARAWERA 100 MILE ENDURANCE RUN

164KM | 100MI • D+ 5,000M | 16,404FT

- ✚ Maori heritage!
- ✚ Hot springs, waterfalls, mountains...
- ✚ Ultra, but doable climbing-wise

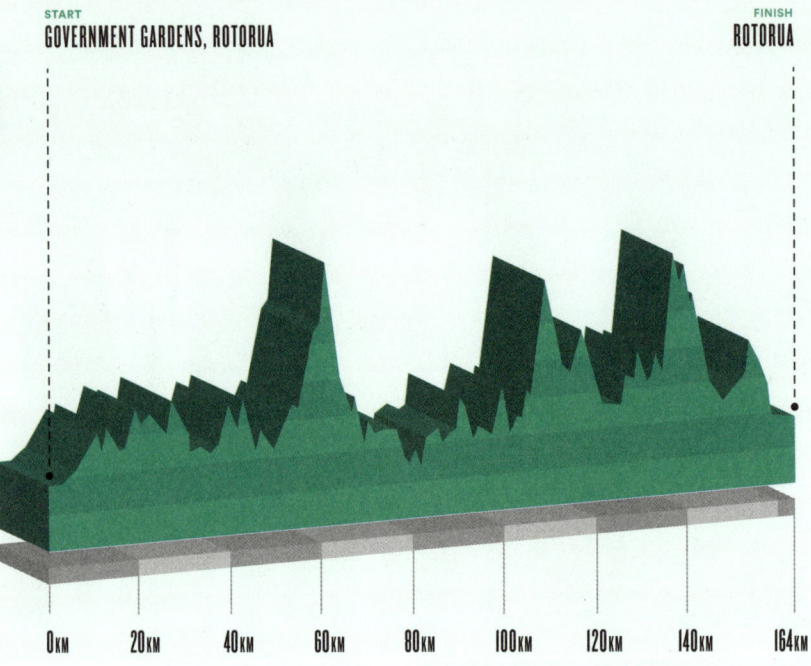

START
GOVERNMENT GARDENS, ROTORUA

FINISH
ROTORUA

0KM 20KM 40KM 60KM 80KM 100KM 120KM 140KM 164KM

OTHER DISTANCES

TARAWERA 62KM COURSE
62KM | 38.5MI • D+ 1,603M | 5,259FT

TARAWERA 87KM COURSE
87KM | 54MI • D+ 2,262M | 7,421FT

TARAWERA 102KM COURSE
102KM | 63.4MI • D+ 2,720M | 8,924FT

JENNIFER GALE

Age 47 • Business operator
Ormeau • Australia

Why did you choose this race?

JENNIFER "Until I was 36, I hardly did any sport. Yes, I swam as a teenager, but it wasn't really my thing. I guess that as a teenager I didn't think it cool to really kill myself. I didn't start running until I was in my thirties, when I challenged myself to move a bit more. I started like everyone else. First 3 kilometres, then 6 kilometres... After eight months' building up, I was ready for a 14-kilometre street run. There were over 60,000 people taking part. I remember well just how impressed I was. Then it went downhill again. Not that I found running boring, but after those 14 kilometres, I didn't do anything for five years. But then I got myself together again. I started with a triathlon. Longer and further, in other words. Then it became clear that I don't really care for asphalt. In the long run, it becomes boring to grind the miles in this way. With trails, you have to jump over a tree trunk or wade through a river from time to time. You may catch sight of a giant spider or a snake slithering away from your feet. You have to watch where you step and that forces you to focus more. Am I becoming long-winded? To cut a long story short: three years ago I ran my first 50 kilometres with a friend, and the following year my first 100 kilometres. Last year I ran that 100 kilometres again. Then there was a big storm during the race, so heavy that just nine out of fifty participants made it to the finishing line. At such events, you quickly make friends. Well, and what then? *Things you do when you've had too many drinks...* Someone talked about the Tarawera Ultramarathon, I saw pictures of it and I was immediately sold!"

How did you prepare?

JENNIFER "For me it was an exercise to train consistently, because I'd registered for the longest distance of the event. Running 100 kilometres is one thing, 165 another (laughs). I was simply not that experienced. I tried to do a long trail race every weekend, to build up my endurance. But in moderation, because I was afraid of injuring myself if I built up too quickly. In the end, my longest training for the Tarawera Ultramarathon was a 6-hour training session. That's not so extreme now, is it? Ultimately, it's simply the frequency of training that counts, no? The only downside in my preparation was that it's pretty flat where I live, while the Tarawera Ultramarathon has around 5,000 metres of vertical climb in addition to the 164 kilometres. But if you compare that with other international races of the same calibre, such as the

Race secret

New Zealand also means Maori. And Maori also means haka. But the native New Zealand population has more to offer than this war dance. Keep your eyes open during the Tarawera Ultramarathon opening ceremony. Definitely not to be missed!

UTMB®, the climbing isn't that bad. Ah, in the end you always have to row with the oars you have."

How did your race go?

JENNIFER "Fine, it was super. The route is so diverse. One moment you're running alongside a lake, half an hour later through a forest, then you pass a spectacular waterfall and then a steaming hot water source. It's the variety that makes this race what it is. I also remember well the aid stations. Even though the race takes place in February, at one supply post all the volunteers were dressed as Santa Claus. Hilarious! Another supply post had disco music as a theme. You run through the wilderness for hours on end, all on your own, and then you bump into a party like that. Things like that give you tons of energy. The social aspect of the trail community was new to me as a rookie. Everyone looks after everyone. Your name is also on your starting number. Everyone calls to

you on the way. That makes an impression. You feel just like a world-famous rock star. I was also happy with my time. I'd set 17 hours as my objective, by ultimately finished in 15 hours 30 minutes. (grins)"

Which moment will you never forget?

JENNIFER "Maybe it's a cliché, but the last five kilometres were the hardest. Someone shouted to me from the trailside that it was just ten minutes or so to the finish. You then work on that basis, but it was not so. I still had 3 to 4 kilometres to go and everyone who has already done an ultra knows that those last kilometres are really rough. It was in the middle of the night and therefore pitch black. I simply wanted to get it behind me. (laughs) That being said, you quickly forget such things. Meanwhile, I'm contemplating registering for the Great Wall Marathon. The course runs across the Great Wall of China. Not a trail race, but some tough climbing!"

A golden tip for future participants?

JENNIFER "Absolutely! During my training period, I chose not to eat meat or processed food. I noticed that I recovered faster by following this diet. Strongly recommended."

"The barefoot Maori warrior, performing during the Welcoming Ceremony in front of the runners, may unwittingly have started a new trend of guys' skirts in ultrarunning."

Sarah Lavender Smith

RUNNING COACH & FINISHER TARAWERA ULTRAMARATHON 2015

GOD

I've fallen apart and lie in pieces on my bed. The only person I saw yesterday and the day before yesterday was my baker around the corner. The church tower strikes the hour. I count the dull strokes because I lack the energy to look at my clock radio. It's three in the afternoon and hot in my penthouse apartment.

That boy needs therapy, psychosomatic
That boy needs therapy, purely psychosomatic
That boy needs therapy.

"Go hiking at least," my psychologist says. "The endorphins will do you good!"

Hiking? But I'm a runner! Actually, he's right, but I remain amorphous. I know, because I've read enough about it. Running works in the case of depression and related ailments, but who helps me don my running shoes?

The Black Dog itself?

Hiking?

To Santiago de Compostela or something like that? A long meditative journey? As my mother did at the time. I stood there as an adolescent watching her take her backpack. My mother, solo, 806 kilometres. How did she manage it?

I stare numbly at the ceiling. Joggers pass by on the quayside. I hear the rhythmic steps of their sports shoes over the cobblestones.

Lie down on the couch! What does that mean? You're a nut! You're crazy in the coconut!

"Let go", my psychologist says.

A break-up - I had a girlfriend in my running club. I don't think I'm going too far when I say I'm going head-under. If you share the same passion and running family, what do you do when the roads separate?

The sharpest knives have two cutting edges.

Last year I went quite deep. I took a career break from my office job and jumped into the deep end as a freelancer. I made a documentary on a mini-budget, directed a cultural event and played freelance editor in a human interest programme. Without a financial plan or too many savings. My trail running was at a low level, because I set the bar high. Working through the night because it was the only way. Pitching at the public broadcaster? Recharge yourself and hope for a water jump to prove yourself. Besides being impetuous, maybe I was naive too? Partly unconsciously incompetent and pretty perfectionist? Too independent-ly-minded? Dealing with rejections has always been a difficult and sensitive business for me. Or am I able, as a semi-millennial, simply to make difficult artistic compromis-es? In Nepal, I found some stillness in soli-tude, but also fuel for crippling brooding in every area of life.

Did I ever tell you the story about cowboys, midgets, And the Indians and frontier psychiatrist?

The doorbell rings.

I don't get up to answer it.

You are what you do and you do what you are.

If I'm not a creative, not an entrepreneur, not a lover, and no longer a trail runner, what am I still? Self-chosen isolation, too many changes at once and a flat battery.

*I felt strangely hypnotised
I was in another world, a world of 20,000 girls
And milk!*

MY KINGDOM IS TOTTERING

The most original advice I received? Every day cook a hot meal for yourself and mas-turbate once. Who's grabbing my hand?

Figuratively.

'After the hours-long, sometimes days-long hormone rush of a heavy race, the Black Dog can lie in wait. It's tough work exam-ining those dark emotions. The thoughts dance in your head like possessed garden equipment, as if a cracked record is turn-ing. The exhaustion washes away every defence. I'm far too familiar with the dark side of emotions to suggest that the Black Dog can become your best friend. The only thing that seems to help is to set off running again. Maybe those post-race emotions are as much a part of a race as training kilo-metres? What if we were to embrace those negative emotions? After an ultra, stripped of all masks, you are so receptive to self-ex-amination that it would be idiotic not to do anything with it. There are more than enough writers, poets, artists and musicians who have made the Black Dog their muse.'

Slumping into the ropes after a race and how a trail runner deals with it. Normally *Darkness*, a YouTube short documentary by Australian trail runner Tegyn Angel offers me perspective and comfort, but this time it's not working.

I'm empty.

*Can you think of anything else that talks, other than a person?
Uh oh, uh oh, a bird! Yeah!
Sometimes a parrot talks.*

GOD ALMIGHTY

In a few months, I'll visit my mother in Egypt. She's working there for a Belgian construction company. Two weeks after that I'll be forced to pick up the thread again on my office job. I've known for a long time that the job doesn't fully suit me, but I need a compelling reason to get out of my bed. And money, because financially I seem to be drowning.

Ha ha ha ha ha!
Yes, some birds are funny when they talk
Can you think of anything else?
A record, record, record!

How do you stop a vortex of brooding?

The place where my mother lives in Cairo is currently her home, not ours. Our home no longer exists since my parents' divorce. I'm thirty-something, but long for the security of the room I had as an adolescent. With all this brooding, I'm not sleeping well. In an attempt to tire myself, I'll eventually don my running shoes, but not wholeheartedly.

"Anger is also a form of sadness," my psychologist said. "And well, Rik, you're not God the Father, are you?" he echoed.

My mother will do her best to distract me, but will crash into my wall, which in turn will lead to frustration on her part. I'll burst into tears.

"What are you doing here in Egypt?" I'll ask, snivelling.

"But Rik, it's not like you came visiting every weekend. Was I to sit waiting?"

How do you shout when you've lost your own voice? ▲▲

Nepal

EVEREST
TRAIL
RACE®

160ᴋᴍ | 100ᴍɪ • 6 sᴛᴀɢᴇs • D+ 14,790ᴍ | 48,523ꜰᴛ

"All roads
end in Jiri.
From now on
it's 99.9%
single track
to the finish."

Martin Schneekloth

WWW.ULTRAKRAUTRUNNING.COM

STORM

In a bar yet again. This time not in *Bidegorri*, my former regular drinking hole, but in the *Taberna Txanton* in the mountain village of Zegama. I'm with my father visiting the part of Spain where I was an Erasmus student some ten years ago.

It's only the second time in my life that I'm travelling alone with him. It's not going too well, but only a small percentage of the reason lies in our intergenerational understanding and differing expectations. Today I need to clear the fog in my head. We cut a deal yesterday. I get my mountains, while he spends the afternoon with a novel and a camera wandering through some country villages.

"Are you mad? Do you see that mist outside? Maybe it's snowing up there!"

Actually, the bartender is right. Even by Basque standards, it's a rotten day. Rain bucketing down and a cold, harsh wind. No weather for a dog. Fortunately, my father hasn't enough Spanish to follow what he's saying. I try to appease. For alpine conditions I've packed long running trousers, gloves and a hat. I have a map with the route, which is also marked with bright yellow spheres on trees and rocks.

Smartphone? Check.

Energy gels, granola bars, sports drinks and water? Check.

Deep-profile trail running shoes? Check.

The bartender sighs. Some old curs at the counter turn their eyes back to their glasses of *patxaran*. I persevere and continue my preparations. I'm not really in top condition, but I have to go into these mountains. It's the only thing that really gets me moving again. All other stimuli are still bogged down too much in noise and dust blowing through my head.

I make a clear agreement with my father. It's now 13:30. If I'm not back at the *Taberna Txanton* by 17:30, he can expect a message saying where I am. If he's heard nothing from me by 18:30, he should sound the alarm. I nod and throw my running backpack over my shoulders.

"Good run! And later together, *dos cervezas*, OK?"

I close the door with the red-white Athletic Bilbao poster behind me. Actually, it's all the fault of a YouTube overdose that I'm here. Running is a craft here. Every spring this massif, with the four highest peaks of the Basque Country, forms the stage for the *Zegama-Aizkorri Mendi Maratoia* - a 42 km mountain marathon with 2,750 metres of climb and an equal amount of descent. My idol Kilian Jornet has won here seven times.

I join the route halfway. From the rock church of Santi Espiritu, I still have twenty-three kilometres with about 800 metres of ascent and 1,500 metres of descent, if I'm to believe my topographic map. Hands on thighs and push. Into the mist, in the direction of grey limestone. With the heavy breathing, the tension in my chest also disappears.

"*Zegama is Zegama*," Kilian Jornet murmurs in my head.

How must it be like here on the race day itself? The flanks of Aratz, Aizkorri, Aitxuri and Andraitz, full of roaring men with misty beards and generous women with leather drinking bottles full of apple cider.

"*Venga, venga! Venga, tío! Aupa! Ánimo!*"

My only companions are a few rain-sodden longhaired sheep among the rocks.

AURRERA BETI!

I wrote the wishes of barman Mikel yesterday on a beermat in *Bidegorri* - my favourite pub in Bilbao. *Siempre adelante*, he translated, always forward! Javi nodded in agreement from under his smoke-filled walrus moustache. My Basque replacement father strengthened the wish with another penultimate round.

This bar has no last rounds, which bring bad luck. In my first months of Erasmus I quickly learned that people don't use *última* but *penúltima* when they talk about *una ronda*.

While pouring the next glass of Rioja, Javi grabs my father's shoulder. The ashes of his cigarette whirl over his costume pants.

"Are you mad? Do you see that mist outside? Maybe it's snowing up there!"

"Explain to me ... You've an analytical head as an architect and politician. Your son is a boisterous poet, who blows in with his backpack every so many years. How is it you're so different?"

Javi shrieks it out. He sees from my eyes that I've not seen the question coming. Meanwhile, Mikel is also hanging curiously over the counter. All eyes are now on my father. I've no idea what he'll answer.

My father occasionally calls me scornfully an eternal boy scout. He knows he will get me on my high horse with it. Actually, he has no idea how often I've already put my head on the block with all kinds of projects. Ever since that newspaper I sold on the playground as a seven-year-old. It may not be his recipe, but we undeniably have a number of ingredients in common.

MR BEER-BELLY AND DADDY BEER-BELLY

"It's my turn to pay the round."
  "No, it's my round!"
  "No, no, it's me who's paying!"

Under the layer of social varnish he's more sensitive than he can sometimes express in words. Maybe I'm sick in the same bed. Somewhere I think we both want to be understood in one way or another. That we seek recognition, perhaps most of all from each other.

He sips his glass and looks me deep in the eyes.

"Tell them it's not so *blanco-negro* ..."

This is no paternalistic ducking-the-question answer. We are both dreamers. Possibly fantasists with a mission. This type of people are driven, but also vulnerable in their utopias and at times on an island.

I stop and look for the drinking nozzle from my water bag. Before I can drink, I have to calm my breathing. So steep ... This is coming close to rock climbing!

SKYRUNNING

The story of this route is now history. In the early nineties, well-known Italian mountaineer Marino Giacometti and some friends explored the possibilities of races on Mont Blanc and Monte Rosa. Running at locations above 2,000 metres with an incline of at least 30% and limited technical climbing is now called *skyrunning*.

With the support of sports brand Fila, this new sports branch quickly grew into an international circuit. Mount Kenya, Mexican volcanoes and Himalayan peaks came under the running shoe. A few intermediate steps eventually led to the establishment of the *International Skyrunning Federation* in 2008 - with *Zegama-Aizkorri Mendi Maratoia* as a permanent fixture on the race agenda.

At the top of Aizkorri, I take shelter under the roof of Santa Cruz church. I dive into my gloves. Not just because of the cold, but also to avoid wounds. The sharp rocks are very slippery. I take another sip of water and plough on to Aitxuri, the next peak of this narrow mountain ridge. I check the altitude on my sports watch.

544 metres climbed.

Is the worst behind me?

Twenty minutes later I dive into the mist. These steep slopes are not made to stay upright on. When I lose my footing a third time on the slippery grass, I admit I'm beaten. Interval. I take off my running backpack and grab a bottle of sports drink and a muesli bar.

No view. In front of me, one mist bank follows another. A silent film, in which even the rattling of the projector is missing.

Here I am.

All alone.

I feel very vulnerable, but with each breath, I also feel a bit more connected to myself. My protective scales are somewhere down in the valley. Perhaps a person finds more inspiration in the elements than in others of his kind?

"Perhaps a person finds more inspiration in the elements than in others of his kind?"

In the grazing land between Olitze and Urbia, I take out my smartphone. A message for my father that I've covered just ten kilometres so far, but that I'm coming close to the final climb. And after that it's 12 kilometres downhill on wide forest trails. So no worries. I press 'send' but the phone refuses. No signal, it turns out. This massif may be a protected nature reserve, but surely it's still in Europe and not a developing country?

I stumble on and take my last energy pellet. The climb to Andraitz must not be less than the two previous peaks. Even though it's only 250 metres, they completely exhaust me. The carved-out steps at the top seem like the antechamber to hell. My head's spinning.

TOO LATE

It's 16:56.

No, I'm not going to make my rendezvous with my father. I fish my smartphone from my backpack to resend the message to my father. This time I have a signal, but with all the fog, rain and sweat, my phone is now soaked. My fingers meander over the display. Nothing reacts. What should I do now?

I search my running backpack for something dry, but there's nothing. An alternative? I tug a thick lump of moss from between the rocks. I squeeze out all the moisture and use the green mass as a natural sponge to dry my smartphone screen.

I press send. Almost at the same time my smartphone stops working.

Goddamnit!

17:18.

Still 12 kilometres to go. I leave the last rocks behind me and blast into the forest. A jumble of beech, oak and birch fly past my eyes. Two more times I stop and repeat the moss ritual, but every time my battery gives up the ghost before I can send the message to my father.

My plan to walk this course was an innocent but self-centred *idée fixe* that now seems to be causing a trail of problems. Because of me, someone who likes to see me is very worried at the moment.

I move up a gear - even though my thighs are killing me. My sports watch indicates 17 kilometres an hour. A few more turns, and a deer with majestic antlers runs out from behind a tumbledown forester's house. I surge past, the beast remains standing in its tracks.

18:05.

I feel asphalt under my feet again. At the end of the street I see Zegama church. Where's my father? I hope he understands. I've just run the most beautiful half marathon of my life, but my first words will be a *mea culpa*.

In front of the *Taberna Txanton* I switch off my sports watch. No trace of my father. While I catch my breath, the bartender comes out with a large, full glass. He looks more than surprised.

"You've come from up there?"
  "Euh, sí ..."
  "And you're back already? That's fast!"
  "Ah, thanks. *Eskerrik asko*!"
  "But the official ending line is on the other side of the church, you know! *Aupa, venga*!"

I get myself moving again and run *pro forma* fifty metres further. Just when I've put my hands up for the bartender, I spot my father on the other side of the square. I spurt towards him.

His face looks worse than a thunderstorm.

"Dammit, Rik! When are you going to learn to take account of others? And aren't you exaggerating with that running?" ▲▲▲

STORM

Hong Kong
VIBRAM
HONG KONG
100 ULTRA TRAIL RACE

Some people almost knowingly
run themselves into injury!

Hong Kong
VIBRAM HONG KONG 100 ULTRA TRAIL RACE

97.4km | **60.5**mi
D+ 4,830m | **15,846**ft

- ⊕ One of Asia's oldest ultra-trails
- ⊕ 80% of the trails are in protected nature areas
- ⊕ The accessibility, diversity and chaos of world city Hong Kong

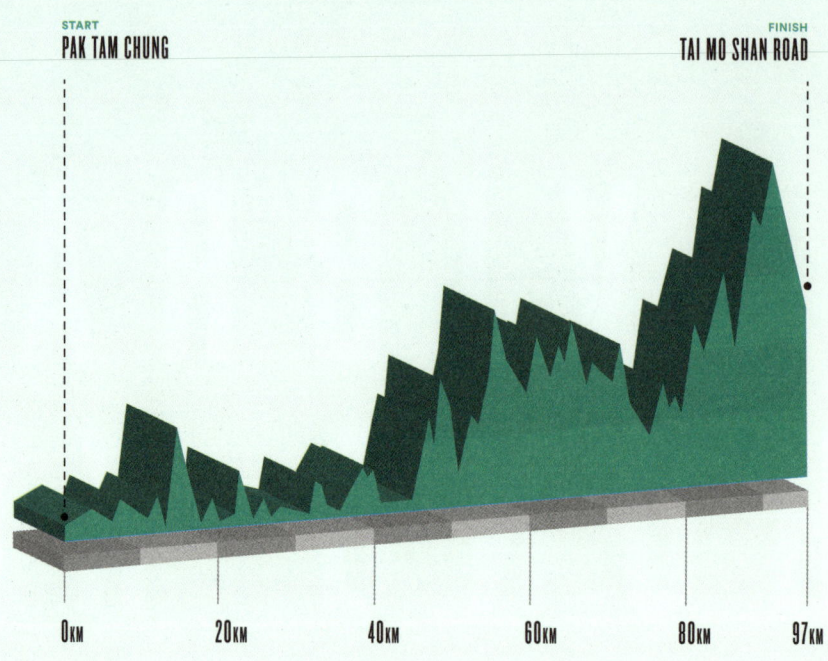

START
PAK TAM CHUNG

FINISH
TAI MO SHAN ROAD

0km   20km   40km   60km   80km   97km

KRIS VAN DE VELDE

Age 40 • Race director cycling and running races Zele, Belgium • Beijing, China

Why did you choose this race?

KRIS "I don't tell a lie when I say that I ended up there by accident. Professionally, one of my jobs is as race director and promoter for races in the Asia Trail Master Championship. A complex job with 34 races in 16 countries! So I'm in the trails world, though I'm not a pure long-distance runner. I did a lot of cycle racing up to five years ago. After that, I did little owing to my busy job. Yes, I took part once in the Ultrabericus, an Italian trail with 66 kilometres and 2,500 metres vertical climb. That went pretty well, as I've been doing sports all my life. So what happened? In my work in the Asia Trail Master Championship, I came into contact with a certain Janet Ng. She's not only race director for the Vibram Hong Kong 100 Ultra Trail Race, but also the Asia officer for the International Trail Running Association (ITRA). It was in that capacity that I wanted to contact her. She promptly invited me to take part in her race. It was the last registration day, so it was just possible. And yes, my number came up in the lottery, it just had to, and now it was up to me (laughs). This race is also a true classic, like the Milan-San Remo in cycling. 1,500 participants from over 30 countries. The purists will say there's too much asphalt, but that's perhaps inevitable on country trails so close to one of the world's most densely populated cities. There is a local movement now too to avoid using asphalt on the trails, but in the old days asphalt was popular to make the routes between rural villages easier to to navigate and maintain. In addition, I simply wanted to experience it, because ultras are something special here. In my job, it struck me that I was always seeing the same faces at events. One weekend an ultra, the next weekend another, and the following weekend again. Some runners almost voluntarily run themselves into injury. Such fanatical runners are rarely seen in the West. Endurance sports are not really part of the Asian psyche, except in Japan. Really fast runners are not grown here. Why then are ultra-trails and other extreme sports events becoming increasingly popular here? I believe it has something to do with its being a way of venting frustration. In communist China, everyone is supposed to be the same. At the same time, there is a lot of envy and jealousy. Anyone sticking his or her head above the parapet gets it cut off. I see lots of people channel their tensions through all kinds of extreme sports. It almost literally comes down to running away from your

Race secret

Don't expect razor-sharp mountain ridges or very technical descents on the Vibram Hong Kong 100 Ultra Trail Race. The course is littered with long flights of stairs with thousands of steps. Like it or hate it, you have to go over them.

problems. Not only in China, but also more generally in the less individually oriented East. Ultra-trails as a safety valve for standing out from the crowd? For me, this is much of what they are about."

How did you prepare?

KRIS "After registering, I had four months to prepare. Apart from that one ultra-trail in Italy, I had no experience with long distances. I didn't really follow a special training plan. Every morning, I spent an hour on the bike trainer. Running was limited to two or three training sessions per week, each lasting no more than one hour. After two months of this regime, I took part in the Frankfurt Marathon. I completed it in 3 hours and 22 minutes. This told me that my basic condition was definitely still good. In the last two months, I also did my best to pay attention to my diet. The last training weeks fell in the Christmas period. I had to pass up on a lot of good things."

How did your race go?

KRIS "You need to know that this race takes place in the winter, because in the summer it's tropically hot in Hong Kong. When I stood on the starting line in 2016, it turned out very wintery. With a stiff wind blowing, it felt like -10°C. As a Belgian, I'm used to this, but the Asians were really shivering. The race itself went smoothly. Almost every 10 kilometres you have a supply point. These keep you knowing where you are. Only after 45 kilometres does it start to get rough, with a lot of up and down. At around 80 kilometres, you go up via Needle Hill and Grassy Hill to Tai Mo Shan, the highest point of the course. The venom of this race is really in the tail. On the way to the highest point, it even started to snow and freeze. On the top of Tai Mo Shan, you couldn't move for people. Not supporters, but people wanting to see the snow, because it's so rare in Hong Kong. Finally, I got to the finish in 20 hours and 18 minutes. The extreme weather

conditions meant that the race was stopped 2 hours later. It had just become too dangerous. 180 people had to be evacuated from the course. A good thing that I finished on time! It was my first and only 100 kilometres until now. I could do it again for a faster time, but that's not what matters to me. A repeat would be a weak decoction of what I'd been through."

Which moment will you never forget?

KRIS "About 3 kilometres before the finish, I was running in a little group with five other runners. We've just finished the last and toughest climb of the race. We can almost smell the finishing line. What can still go wrong? The road surface was slippery with black ice, but we didn't see that. We all fell over at the same time. All crashed onto the ground, like straight out of a Disney cartoon!"

A golden tip for future participants?

KRIS "Don't follow my example. Prepare well. Keep enough energy for the second half of the race. Normally you start it when the night is falling. This is an extra difficulty, for which you need a clear head. The race is doable, but despite my sports history I was more than tired. This year, I ran the Paris Eco-Trail carrying too much weight. I managed those 80 kilometres on sheer dogged determination, but sufficient training kilometres ensure that you know mentally beforehand that you will succeed."

"It's not how you start that matters. It's how you finish."

RACE REPORT HK 100 ON ULTRA168.COM

FAR WEST

"Dear travellers, the 7:46 am train to Brussels will be delayed by 12 minutes. We apologize for this."

Despite my coffee and newspaper, my shorts and bright red Salomon shoes make me a strange duck among the commuters. I'm travelling to Brussels, yes, but not routinely to the administrative district round the North Station, but on to Comblain-au-Pont. I've recently started, on my days off, running sections of the GR 57, a 240-kilometre walking trail through the Ardennes. Looking for Belgium-without-concrete, far away from the office.

Two transfers and three newspaper sections later I get started on my midweek anti-poison. Brain offline. Follow the red and white stripes which mark the Grande Randonnée. Instinct online. Over the railway tracks, past some last straggling houses and into the forest. Immediately uphill. I slither with small steps. The first mud splashes on my calves feel fresh. Three puddles later I already have wet feet. Actually, I don't know from where I get the strength to start.

Running through forests on weekdays is very different from competitions.

Somehow you constantly tell yourself that it's very normal to go running in the woods on your own, at the same time you also hear a voice in your head that claims the opposite. Striking also how nature reacts. A swarm of hundreds of runners is a sponge that sucks all the nuance out of a forest. On my own, I can hear the twigs cracking under my soles and I start as birds fly up. In the absence of distraction from other runners, I'm amazed by sagging clumps of moss, misty mushrooms and the smooth, pearly shine of wet slate. Maybe this is trail running in its purest form? Do I, just as a real smoker opts for heavy Groene Michel cigarettes without filters, also find my freedom in being restricted by my two feet only?

APERO

Passing along a track I bump into a red warning sign. It's hunting season and I'm stuck: no access until 11:00 am. I've been on the train for more than 2.5 hours and am now faced with the invisible closed level crossing of the arm of the law. I look at my watch. It's 10:38 am. I've no wish to catch a stray bullet. There's nothing for it other than to wait. I take off my running backpack, take out my fleece and squat down.

I scan the surroundings. No living creature in sight. I went to the forest to feel raw and wild, but bumped again into bureaucracy. It seems as if my job is correcting me, because a weekday is and will remain a working day in this country.

I count down the last minutes. A roaring noise makes me look up. A heavy jeep slowly rolls out of the woods like a tank. A fat man with a hat behind the wheel. Half-open window. I get up and ask him if the coast is clear. He nods vaguely and says uninterestedly that I have to wait for his fellow hunters, who are coming on foot. The platform is empty. Bad hunting or work in progress?

The jeep disappears from view. Even before the roar of the engine has completely disappeared, I hear barking dogs. The forefront of the hunters. A few minutes later they are standing in a circle around me.

"Eleven o'clock. Apéritif time!"

The jeep returns with a crate of Jupiler beer. Without explanation a bottle is pushed into my hands. In these woods you don't drink isotonic water, just beer. We toast. To the hunt, to the journey. And to Dame Fortune, because this morning they didn't shoot a single animal. They will immediately comb a second forest, I hear. While tipping back the last gulps, I ask one of the hunters why he's carrying a heavy wooden staff with a strange metal attachment. His eyes light up. From the leather sheath at his hip he takes a long bayonet and clicks it onto the attachment. He explains to me that they finish off game in this way when it's not dead immediately. A single push, more effort is not required. The weapon's shaft is thick with dried blood.

I take a last sip. Just now they told me they'd not shot anything yet. So where does that blood come from? I fall right into the trap.

"Maybe this is trail running in its purest form?"

"It's my mother-in-law's! She wasn't completely dead!" the bayonet's owner brags.

The group toasts to that. From the last hunting season, it turns out. Black humour doesn't rust. And certainly not in this corner of the Ardennes. Belching loudly, I continue my path.

LOUISE

Two weeks ago, I did things a little differently. I made it a three-day affair instead of a day trip. Without overnight reservations. Coincidence brought me for the first night to the presbytery of Eusebius, a parish priest from Africa. A glass of port, a sturdy plate of spaghetti and a spare room. Night two drove me into the arms of Louise. I wanted to take on water again for the final climb to La Roche-en-Ardenne, but the village had no café. I rang at the door. A drowned-out old woman opened, in the company of two dogs and a handful of cats.

"I've only got wine!" she replied.

A stove glowed in the distance. I was cold and it was no longer far to the tourist hole of La Roche-en-Ardenne, where I was hoping to find bed-bath-bread.

"OK, then we drink wine!"

"Haha! *Entrez*, comrade!"

On pouring the fourth glass of wine, Louise confessed to me that she had doubted whether to ask me in, but she had made a promise to herself and wanted to stick to it. Her adventures as café-boss in Brussels, the life story of her deceased husband and the late coming-outs of her two homosexual sons had already been recounted. Clearly not only the animals talk in the forest.

"A few years ago two scouts stood here at the door. Twelve or thirteen years old. Just like you, they asked for water. I went to the kitchen to fill their jerrycan. When I returned, there was a third man. And he wasn't thirteen..."

Louise took a swig. She looked at me. Her eyes shot fire.
"They knocked out my teeth for 32 euros. They threw my dogs against the wall and destroyed everything. And when it turned out that I really had nothing valuable in the house, they said they'd piss on me."

I swallowed hard.
"I woke up in the hospital. In retrospect, it turned out that the young people were from a youth detention centre in Mons. They were minors, and they were not punished."

I wondered where she had gathered the courage to let me in. The answer quickly arrived.

"I've only got wine."

"Actually, I'm grateful to those kids, because I really don't fear anything anymore. I went to a psychiatrist twice after that attack. It was that or go mad. And I'm not going to give those young people the pleasure. There's no one who can still frighten me now!"

Glass of wine number five. In the meantime, it was pitch dark. Actually I was too drunk to crawl to La Roche-en-Ardenne. For Louise it was no problem to lend her sofa for a night to an unknown traveller passing through. It also turned out to be a reason to really start the party. She donned a long skirt and took me to a hidden pub in the village.
"This one is only open in the evenings, when all hikers and mountain bikers are gone," she confided.

We opened the door. There they were. The local postman, bus driver, teacher and forester - also a hunter. All in the singular. Louise ordered more wine. I flew to the beer. It loosened tongues. I learned that the forest keeper-gamekeeper was a crossbow hunting fan. An authentic but also silent way to get game on a plate. And certainly outside the hunting season, because a man from time to time can earn a penny in the black, right?

When Louise fell from her bar stool and could barely get straight again, it was fine by me. I heaved her arm over my shoulder and pulled her over the bridge. Back in her house she hurried to the chest of drawers next to the stove.
"I didn't tell you, but there's another reason I'm not afraid anymore," she said.

From the middle drawer she drew a shiny revolver.

I turn into a new winding path. In front of me, two fawns shoot out of the wood. Their eyes fix mine. I seem to have a patent on these animals. They freeze. I don't move either. Through the foliage I see the contours of a powerful antler. Father stag, who also doesn't know what to do. I'm having more luck than this morning's hunters. Maybe I should buy a weapon and take shooting lessons? I have little time to fantasize. The young deer dive away. Back into the womb of the forest.

With a grin I start the descent into the valley. I push my earphones in deeper and turn up the volume. Hurray for the positive force of aggression. Thank you the Northern Irish gentlemen of Therapy?.

Fucker!

My tongue is twisted from talking
My feet are blistered from walking alone
My head is bursting with thoughts
And every bruise feels so familiar
This city's buzzing with bastards
Cancer tans and plastic disasters
Wannabees and users and makers
Impotents and shake city fakers.

So don't tell me everything's all right
And don't include me in your straight life
And don't tell me everything's all right
In your straight life.

A quarter of an hour later I switch off my sports watch. The GPS indicates 44 kilometres. Time to take the train back home. On the train I wrap myself in a dry fleece, pull my legs up and fall asleep.

No suffering without pain. ▲▲▲

I was scared to death: "*Putain*! How did you get that?"

Purchased from the suitcase of a Russian underworld figure, who rang and asked her if she couldn't use a gun, it turned out. Poaching and illegal arms sales... Is this Belgium or the Far West? I wondered what other dark secrets this valley still held. I was almost at my limit when I snuggled into the sofa. A few hours later I was woken up by the clatter of Louise peeing over a pink bucket containing more excreta than just urine. I was disgusted. What was I actually doing here like a lonely cowboy without a horse? Maybe it was time to train again in a conventional way?

I chase away the image of Louise with her legs apart and concentrate on the path again. I've been on the road for over 5 hours. I'm almost through my supply of concentrate. The sun seems to be going down. How far is that station? The tree roots that pierce the path bang brutally into my foot bones.

South Africa
ULTRA-TRAIL CAPE TOWN®

I felt more athletic there
than at other races.

Cape Town
ULTRA-TRAIL CAPE TOWN®

65KM | 40MI • D+ 3,000M | 10,170FT

- ⊕ Table Mountain, a rare Unesco world heritage site open to trail runners!
- ⊕ In the middle of a metropolis, with a view of the Atlantic Ocean
- ⊕ Varied terrain & great biodiversity

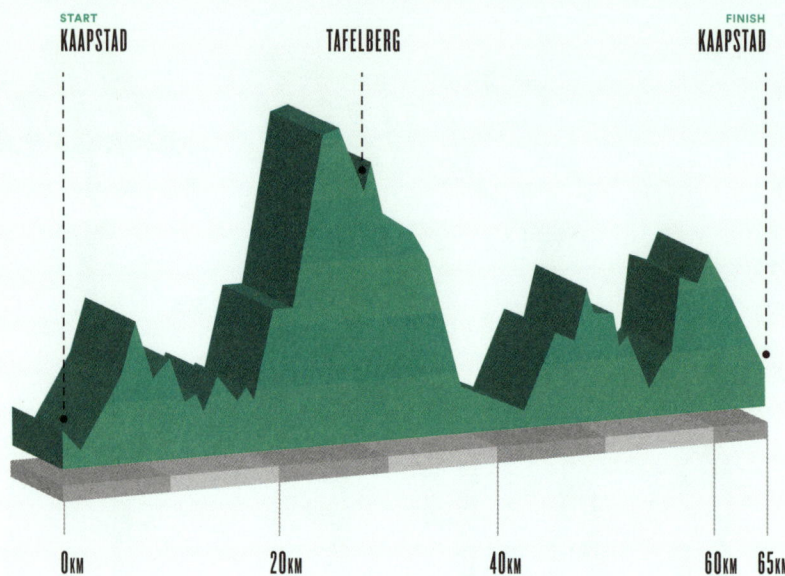

START
KAAPSTAD
TAFELBERG
FINISH
KAAPSTAD

0KM 20KM 40KM 60KM 65KM

OTHER DISTANCES

UTCT® 21KM TRAIL
21KM | 13MI • D+ 1,200M | 3,937FT

UTCT® 35KM TRAIL
35KM | 21.75MI • D+ 2,000M | 6,561FT

UTCT® 100KM ULTRA-TRAIL
100KM | 62.2MI • D+ 4,300M | 14,107FT

BART DE WEIRDT

Age 42 • IT consultant
Ghent • Belgium

Why did you choose this race?

BART "After studying business psychology, I started working at a company where I had the opportunity to train internally as an IT employee. A happy coincidence: I was lucky to be sent to Cape Town for three months' training. At the time the city appealed to me enormously. I suspect this had stuck, but it wasn't the immediate reason why I wanted to run a serious trail. A year before the Ultra-Trail Cape Town® (UTCT®), I'd participated in the Matterhorn Ultraks in Switzerland. I did there the Sky Race with 49 kilometres and 3,600 metres vertical climb. I just missed the cut-off time of the last checkpoint. I guess I wasted too much time on the way in the aid stations. Frustrating, because it would have been my first ultra. I really wanted to know if I could do something like that, physically and mentally. So I went looking for a new challenge with which to test myself again. A running buddy was keen to travel to South Africa, so I started googling and quickly came across the UTCT®. The shortest distance of 35 kilometres seemed too short to justify a trip to the other side of the world. The 100 kilometres was too extreme, but never say never."

How did you prepare?

BART "I'd already scheduled a marathon the same year. So yes, from there it's feasible to build up to a 65 km race. I ran the marathon in 4 hours and 16 minutes. With seven months to the UTCT®, my base was there, but after that it was anything but smooth sailing. After the marathon, I was sick of the whole scene. Pure decompression. When I finally started training properly, I twisted my ankle. Which meant five weeks with no running kilometres. After that, I contacted a professional coach to help me expand my training volume. The training plan consisted, surprisingly, of 30% running and 70% cycling. I also sought more variation in my training. First onto the bike, then climbing on the trails, then back on the bike. Finally, I felt that I was making progress. Until a month and a half before the UTCT®, when fate struck again. I'd enrolled for an obstacle run. I'd trained for something of a much larger calibre. What could go wrong with a 7-kilometre race and twenty obstacles? A lot, as it turned out, because I slipped as I prepared to jump over a little canal. I bruised my knee and by the night, it was as thick as a volleyball. The doctor on weekend duty sent me to the emergency department. I was in trouble again. A few weeks' total rest, just at the most serious point of my training programme. At that stage, I wisely decided to change my registration to the shortest distance. All the more because I was going there with my former girlfriend and we planned a tourist trip with it. It made no sense to miss the rest of the holiday" (laughs).

How did your race go?

BART "At the start, you feel you're taking part in something bigger than you're accustomed to. I'm not talking about the scale of the event, but I nonetheless felt more athletic than at other races. Although it could have been otherwise: I'd forgotten to set my alarm clock. It's terrible to oversleep at such a moment. Luckily, we were staying not far from the start and my equipment was ready, but a quiet breakfast was no longer possible. Initially, I was nervous. Would my knee hold up? But after the first kilometres through the centre and the first uphill sections on Signal Hill I felt that it was OK. Via Lion's Head, we then went up Table Mountain. Unfortunately, with the fog, visibility was zero point zero. It was a bit of a disappointment that my distance went only halfway up Table Mountain and then down again, while the longer distances went right up to the top. Maybe there was a clear sky above the fog banks? So, there you are... it became a UTCT® light. Meanwhile, I still have not run an ultra. And, honestly, that stings. Not that I want to prove myself towards my running buddies, but it feels like unfinished business. It has to do with a sense of honour. Secretly, I would like to call myself an ultra runner, not in order to be part of the club, but to have tested myself. That is why I certainly hope to return. Both to the Matterhorn Ultraks and to a longer distance on the UTCT®. I still have that ultra to my credit! Or to the Otter African Trail Run. In South Africa, they call this marathon *The Grail of Trail*. Can't be bad, can it?"

Which moment will you never forget?

BART "It's perhaps a cliché, but the arrival was fantastic. The last 100 metres were covered with a red carpet. After such a trip through the fog, you feel richer than a king. Especially if your girlfriend's waiting for you at the finishing line. But because I ran the shortest distance, my race was no more than a snack. In the afternoon, we were already tourists in Cape Town. So far the glory of a finisher!" (laughs).

A golden tip for future participants?

BART "Reconnoitre the course the day before the race. With a cable lift, you can go up Table Mountain. It's not skyrunning, but the terrain is quite technical. It can help to have seen it once. As a Belgian, I'm not used to such trails. Without a rekkie, I would not have felt comfortable. Also, provide plenty of time to explore Cape Town and the surrounding area. It's very romantic."

THE HOLY TRAIL

"Ultra distances require training commitment; people ultimately want to be rewarded by racing in iconic destinations, and in Cape Town we have the world's most popular city and running on Table Mountain, a World Natural Wonder, is a hard destination to beat."

Nic Bornman
RACE DIRECTOR UTCT®

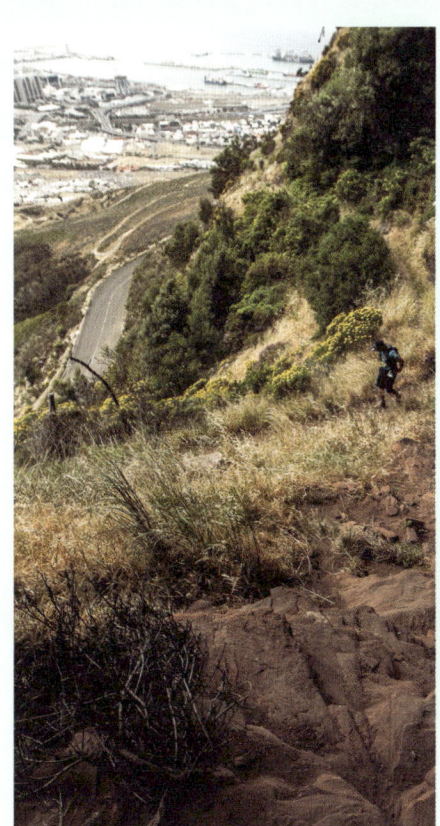

PREGNANT

Goddamnit! Screw it! Monday morning. I thought I'd leave in good time, including breakfast. Not just coffee, but also solid food. Even a piece of fruit. A jumble of hopping rabbits and rabid pheasants on the towpath. Lockkeepers still rubbing the morning out of their eyes and skippers who answer my greeting with a nod from their unwieldy barges. The Scheldt is still evaporating from the night and gathering mists that glide low over the fields.

Another commuting cyclist crosses me. Also smartly clad in proper gear, with a backpack with work clothing. Only then does it dawn on me. I've covered a third of the route in my shower gear with my work clothes still on the kitchen table. I look at my GPS, start calculating and run through my options. Fast home? And then? I don't own a car any more. The train? Nope, by the time I get to the station, it'll be gone.

Rik Merchie, *you dumb monkey*!

Telling them I'm coming later is not an option. I quit my office job in Brussels a few months ago and returned to an old love.

I'm a schoolteacher again, *mijnheer* (Mr) Rik, pronounced variously as *moeneer, menner,* sometimes also *mevrouw* (Mrs) Rik - I have only female colleagues and the students regularly slip up. Education is punctuality, including in a reception class for non-Dutch-speaking newcomers. I experienced this by twice appearing late for lessons. I've exhausted all my credit. In 1 hour and 10 minutes, 15 young people bursting with hormones will be in my classroom. If I'm late, the director will most likely want to see me. Can a teacher be kept in detention?

FORMER RUNNING LEGS

Because you can't miss a bike, like you can miss a train, I leave public transport for what it is. Loudly gasping, I close my front door and I crawl back onto the saddle. I quickly fish two forgotten energy gels with caffeine out of my dusty running gear box, push them down with a sip of water, click myself fast and start pedalling like a madman. Come on, legs, stomp!

Moeneer Rik is no longer a runner. Let alone a trail runner.

A frame between my reduced-to-pulp ex-running legs. 35 flat kilometres one way: not even a marathon. In the distance the wooded hills of the Flemish Ardennes gleam. I miss the game with the winding paths, but I don't make it. On the other hand, my stomach is turning from running-running-running. Is it so bad not to have run a trail race one weekend? The adventurous little online clips on which I once slaked my thirst seem to me irrelevant product placement today. Why should I also reflect those professional athletes? I don't have a sponsored Mercedes Marco Polo motorhome, like Kilian Jornet, to move nomadically from one massif to another.

I feel overtaken by real life and like I'm standing back at the bottom of the ladder. A Sisyphus who has to roll his stone back uphill again.

A young lady in a Belgian cycling championship jersey shoots past me.

"Hey... may... I... slipstream you?"

She gestures that I can. I bend low over my handlebars and dive behind her ass. I scream out of breath something about class, students, too late and problem. No idea if she understood anything about it. I look at her gear apparatus and switch to the smallest gearwheel. The tricolour sweater for me hardly moves. I swing from side to side as I struggle to keep up.

Runners and cyclists have never been a good marriage – leaving aside hybrid duathletes and triathletes. Tell an injured runner that he has to change his running shoes for a bike or the swimming pool and you can guarantee you'll be told where to get off.

Have you ever heard of an injured swimmer raging because his doctor told him to run as an alternative? No, I didn't think so.

According to Ian Corless, photographer and living encyclopaedia of everything that breathes trail running, there are only three types of runners:

the injured runner;
the almost injured runner;
the runner who starts again after an injury.

"Come on, legs, stomp!"

No long-distance runner will deny that long-lasting pounding and banging does something to the lower limbs. Sometimes a few days of rest are enough to ward off emerging aches and pains. At other times - usually in full build-up to the one big race - we break.

If you want to be a good runner, you have to run. But cycling can help you: no impact on those bones, no stress on those tendons. Other benefits: impact-free and active recovery after a tough race or uphill-downhill as interval training, cycling as an extension of your long-distance running. In the saddle you burn only half the calories, but these wretched cycling shoes might spare you a series of sessions with the physiotherapist. And with upright cycling you train the same muscles as running uphill, I read in a trail running manual.

Three bridges and two locks further, my three-coloured saving angel turns around. She shoots off again at 35 kilometres an hour. I have 10 minutes before the bell. Meanwhile, the energy gels have done their work. A chemical lactic taste in my mouth. I pump further, with a particularly aggressive Steak Number Eight song in my ears. The suspicion haunts me that this set of Belgian young wolves will never win the Nobel Peace Prize, but that more than likely this makes no difference to them.

I'm going to burn you down
I am a pyromaniac
I'm going to burn you down.

"Yes, Sirine, I'm pregnant! I'm having a baby."

YOU, BABY?

I slip through the service entrance, drop my bike into an anonymous consultation room and jostle up the stairs between students. On time - or just about. I stamp on towards my classroom. Sirine, born in Tunisia but now East Flemish 3,000 metres athletic champion, leans against the coat racks in the corridor.

"*Menner* Rik, you big belly! You, baby?" she teases.

The rest of the class bursts out laughing. You look so lovely in your Lycra. I know she's dreaming of the Olympics. Every weekday she's on the athletics track at 6 in the morning for interval training.

Welcome back, Mr Beer-Belly!

Been a while…

And how are you?

"Yes, Sirine! I'm pregnant! I'm having a baby! A little child!" I give her tit for tat.

I have a pedantic side. I'm a teacher and this is Dutch for non-native speakers. Therefore, the same message three times. Every time with different words, because every moment can be a learning moment. I shuffle with my smooth click shoes to the desk in front of the blackboard and tell them to turn to page 53 in their workbook. Exercises on coordination and subordination. I also ask them to read a fairy tale themselves and to look up the words they don't understand in a dictionary. When everyone is more or less getting started, I spurt out the class. A cat-lick wash and a change of clothes later I'm back in front of the blackboard.

I take a swig from my bottle and feel myself come back down to earth. The criminal execution in the director's office has been avoided and all sleep was dispelled by the hellish towpath expedition. The world is in my class and today I can handle it.

Done with running. Racing, damn it!

BACKPACK

Tarek, a boat refugee from the Aleppo in Syria, raises his finger. He is busy with the fairy tale and wrestles with the word 'water well'. I make a drawing on the board.

"Ah! That too in my *village*. With heads with blood in it."

It takes a while before I've got the sentence into normal Dutch. My audience knows something about suffering and being on the road. For example, Tarek told me later in Ostend that it was only the second time in his life that he had seen the sea.

"Why the second time?" I asked in sincere amazement.

"First time when I came with little boat from Syria, Mister Rik."

Everyone has an invisible past and ditto backpack. And for one that backpack is a trendy 15 litre laptop bag, for another a 120 litre waterproof duffel bag. For some people their past is an elephants' graveyard they visit occasionally, for others a genocide museum which they have to pass through daily.

Same thing yesterday. Bashir pulled out his smartphone. He had photos for me. From his journey to Belgium, with smugglers from Afghanistan. With his half index finger – truncated by the Taliban, he claims – he glides over the screen. A mountainous desert. No more water. On foot, hunted by sharp-shooting border guards.

"That one dead, that one dead. That too," he points.

Three days on the road in the border country between Iran and Turkey. Or two days and a half. It's not immediately clear to me with the problem with his index finger.

His story reduces selfie-shooting trail runners with running backpacks full of fluids, sugar and salt to infamous control freaks and wannabes with narcissistic or masochistic personality disorders.

John from Nigeria raises his hand. A tree of a guy, with a golden heart. His exercise is about holidays. Sun, sea and beach.

"What you do on holiday, Mister Rik?"
  "I go to the mountains, *Big John*!"
  "The *fountains*?"
  "The *mountains*, *Big John*!" ▲▲▲

Switzerland

MATTER-HORN ULTRAKS

49KM | 30.5MI • D+ 4,500M | 14,763FT

"One of the greatest landscapes for trail running."

Kilian Jornet

France, Italy & Switzerland

ULTRA·TRAIL
DU
MONT·BLANC®

It's a family.

Chamonix
PETITE TROTTE À LÉON (PTL)

290km | 180mi
D+ 26.500m | 86,942ft

⊕ Mont Blanc, baby!

⊕ The World Summit of Trail Running

⊕ High-class organization

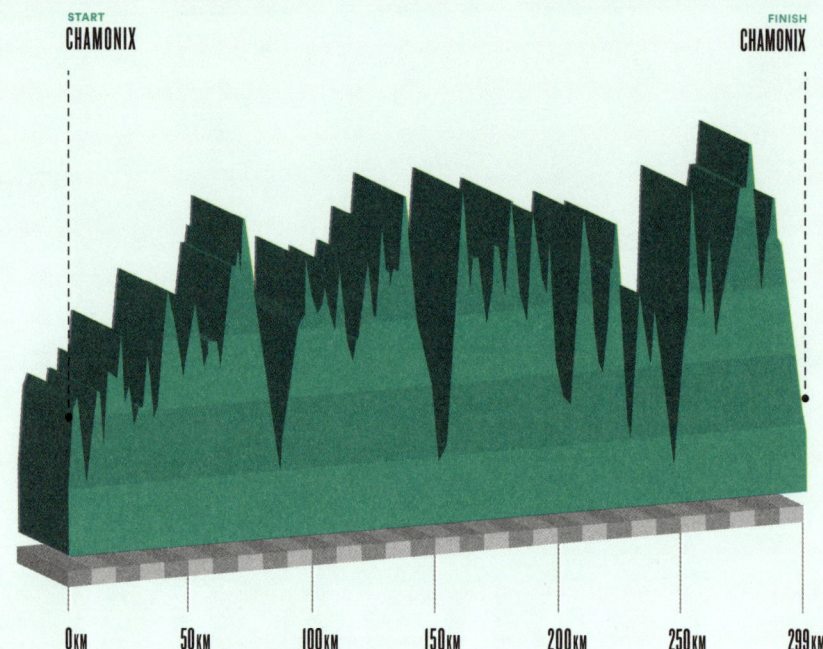

START
CHAMONIX

FINISH
CHAMONIX

0km   50km   100km   150km   200km   250km   299km

OTHER DISTANCES

ORSIÈRES-CHAMPEX-CHAMONIX (OCC)
56km | 34.8mi • D+ 3,500m | 11,482ft

COURMAYEUR-CHAMPEX-CHAMONIX (CCC)
101km | 62.7mi • D+ 6,100m | 20,013ft

SUR LES TRACES DES DUCS DE SAVOIE (TDS)
119km | 74mi • D+ 7,200m | 23,622ft

ULTRA-TRAIL DU MONT-BLANC® (UTMB®)
171km | 106.25mi • D+ 10,000m | 32,808ft

MARIO RAMOS

Age 51 • Professor of Spanish
Lima • Peru

Why did you choose this race?

MARIO "In 2013, I was in Chamonix for the UTMB® for the first time. At that time, I didn't know there were lots of other races apart from the 170 kilometre circuit around the Mont Blanc massif. That's when I first heard about the PTL, one of the four other races that start during the UTMB® week. Every year, a different route of around 290 kilometres and over 25,000 metres of vertical climb. The PTL is also much more technical than the other races. Scrambling over narrow mountain ridges and through snowfields or fields of rough stones. No smooth UTMB® paths (laughs). In addition, there is no first, second or third place. Either you finish or you don't. Also remarkable: the course is not marked. You have to do it yourself with a compass and GPS. Moreover, you don't run this race alone, but together with one or two teammates. You also have to take care of your food and drink on the way, because there are no aid stations provided by the race itself. You go looking for mountain huts for a meal according to your needs. Or for a quick sleep, as this race has no stages. The organization also insists that you carry a lot of material for your own safety. With a minimum of 2 litres of water, a lightweight tent or survival shelter and crampons, you're quickly up to a 6-kilo backpack. In all these aspects, the PTL clearly differs from other long races, such as the Tor des Géants® in the Italian Aosta Valley. I do the PTL not as a competition but as a unique adventure, a party shared with equals. Maybe even a way of life, because since 2014 I've not skipped a year."

How did you prepare?

MARIO "I didn't follow any training plan. I'm not an adrenaline junkie or a top athlete, I'm just someone who likes to take long walks in the mountains. Here in Peru, I often do long hikes in the Andes. Not 3 to 4-hour day trips, but 8 to 9 hours' hard walking. Enjoying nature together with my friends, that's how I found my way into the ultras world. But don't underestimate the PTL. It's a brutal race, and you need to be able to do more than run in the mountains. This is best illustrated by the extensive questionnaire you have to fill in as a candidate. This assesses not just your motivation as a team, but also your experience in mountains. Some questions are very specific. For example, they want to see your list of achievements in recent years, whether you are familiar with crampons and GPS, if you have taken mountaineering training... They also take into account

how you relate to mountains as a natural biotope. They're strict in selecting participants. Which is a good thing. For example, a person may be an excellent marathon runner, but if he's never stood on a glacier or isn't familiar with *via ferrata*, he may endanger himself. Especially after a few days of running, when you've accumulated so much sleep deprivation that you react differently to stimuli. It is therefore necessary to have collectively, as a team, sufficient experience to serve as a safety buffer."

How did your race go?

MARIO "Every year's different. Not only because the course changes, but because each year I ran it with different teammates. The last time I took part was very

special. I started with the PTL, but in the consecutive weeks, I also ran the Ultra Tour Monte Rosa and the Tor des Géants®. A total of 810 kilometres, with 63,500 metres of vertical climb, in 19 days. Did I say that I like running around in the mountains? (laughs) It's not about the numbers or the ego. I just do this for myself, because it does me a power of good. In the end, such ultras are not about your physical condition, but whether you have the willpower to continue. *Will* is more important than top form. A race like the PTL is therefore a very inner, almost intimate experience. Not only because of the challenge, but also because of the emotions you share with your teammates, other participants and the many volunteers.

Race secret

PTL stands for *Petite Trotte à Léon*. Freely translated: the little walk to Léon's place. 300 kilometres is a lot of time to ponder who the fuck this Léon may be. Save your energy for the competition itself, because here is the answer: Léon refers to Lovey Léon, the baker-cum-pastry chef in the Swiss resort of Champex. The first PTL race director, the late mountain guide Jean-Claude Marnier, and his mountain friends were looking for a name for their race. They examined many names for their child, but none felt right. Until suddenly, with *Petite Trotte à Léon*, a sarcastic sobriquet rolled over the table, one everyone felt to be right. Long live mountain humour, *et pour moi deux pains au chocolat et une tarte aux myrtilles, s'il vous plaît*!

The first day you can click perfectly with your teammates, but after a few days without sleep, things can go seriously wrong. Those feelings come up to the surface and you have to be able to live through them. Without wanting to sound elitist: it's an exclusive family feeling that creeps under your skin, but it's not handed to you on a plate."

Which moment will you never forget?

MARIO "I immediately think of my first participation in 2014. The route was at times an elongated waterfall. Also, the spectators in Chamonix are always fantastic. They really pick out the PTL runners from those of all the other races. You can hear that from the applause at the finish zone. The organization itself also contributes to this. At the award ceremony at the end of the UTMB® week, all PTL finishers are called onto the podium. Not the first three, like with the OCC, CCC, TDS and UTMB®, but everyone who finishes. Every time, guaranteed goose pimples with that cling-cling of those little cowbells, which every PTL finisher receives as a souvenir."

A golden tip for future participants?

MARIO "It's always useful to have someone with past PTL experience in your team. It's such a specific race, where field knowledge and competition experience really are a plus."

SUMMER

looked it up again just to be sure. Since 2014, the record of 34 minutes and 18 seconds has been held by – who else? – Kilian Jornet. I look up and follow the zigzagging path under the cable car to Planpraz. One kilometre of vertical climb over 3.8 kilometres. Along a narrow gravel path, with the last 200 vertical metres across steel cables, ladders and steps. The digital clock on the corner of Place de l'Eglise has just shown 33°C. Could they really not have built that cable car without chopping back that shady forest?

My cola in the Bar de Chamonix is a stay of execution. Last week I attended a basic mountaineering course. In the evening I searched the mountain paths to investigate whether my cycling condition was translating to uphill and downhill running without too much puff.

Today comes the big test.

I press the chrono of my sports watch. Off we go.

Just past the gendarmerie I'm already hanging out for the count over my water bag. These temperatures don't match those I'm

used to on the banks of the Scheldt. The last stretches of black asphalt make me feel even hotter. With not a breath of wind in this valley, the fumes of the freight traffic and the many tourists' cars linger in the air, making Chamonix as polluted as Paris.

'Pure air? Not here!' scream graffiti on different walls in this mountain town.

Long live vacation colonies for fresh mountain air?

After four turns of gravel path I stop jogging. Step by step, hands on thighs and pushing. In the hairpin bends, my sweat falls in big drops onto the dusty ground in front of me. I push my earphones deeper for my song of this summer. The song 'My Own Summer' from Deftones sounds almost ironic. With my spare breath I croon:

Cloud, come
Shove the sun aside
Shove it, shove it, shove it.

After 400 metres of vertical, I flop down. Chamonix has become smaller, but the contours of its buildings, residents and visitors are still too clear for my liking.

How does Kilian do it?

I unhook my running backpack and unzip the side pocket in search of an energy gel. Tossing the pack back in place, I tear open the package with my teeth, suck up the sweet nectar and rinse down the mess with some gulps of water.

Come on, Rik!

SPIDERMAN

Three hairpin bends later I see in the distance the foothills of the rock climbing walls of the Aiguille Rouge. I chuckle. How in God's name did I survive that? Dudas, the Hungarian owner of the campsite where I've been camping for a week, is an old fogey of 75. He doesn't really walk anymore, but shuffles. Footnote: in his previous life he was a mountain guide. When I caught him doing gymnastics early in the morning and he was surprised I didn't laugh at him, he asked me if I wanted to go rock climbing. I was too fascinated to say no. 250 metres up. I pointed out that I'd never done anything like this, but it didn't worry him.

From his equipment box he fished me out a belt, a set of snaplinks and a pair of half-worn climbing shoes. He seemed to doubt for a moment.

"Sorry, I've got athlete's foot."

"No problem, me too" I mumble.

Instructions followed at the foot of the rock. Not cautious words with his timid falsetto voice, but powerful, blustering orders. He climbed first and hooked the climbing sets between his rope and the rock. I stood watching wide-mouthed. This old geezer has the flexibility of a grasshopper. What didn't work on the flat he compensated vertically. I stood quivering just 3 metres above ground.

"Allez! Allez! Vite!" came a voice from 9 metres higher.

With difficulty I undid the first snaplink. It's been a long time since I felt so helpless. Saying that I don't dare isn't an option here. The only way is up. When I click in on the resting point and present my fear to him, his answer is as short as it is surprising.

"No need to be afraid … Excuse me, I need to go to the toilet!"

Without further explanation he clicked himself fast to the wall with a strap. With climbing harness off and trousers down he squatted. The sound of an emptying sink followed. Necessity knows no law. He had warned me that this could happen. His doctor once prescribed a wrong antibiotic to him, which shot his intestinal flora to pieces. Five times a day this forced scenario was the result, but he was still going to climb.

Forget New York. Spiderman's grandfather lives in Chamonix.

I put my left foot on the first ladder rung. The variety does me good. How long would it be? Ten minutes? A quarter of an hour? Half an hour? At the top an unexpected icy wind, after which the sun beat down mercilessly on me again. Vertical climbs cause the mercury to drop by 0.6°C per 100 metres and I'm not sorry about that today.

150 metres above the ski lift exit I turn off my sports watch.

1 hour and 26 minutes.

Again: how does Kilian do it?

After some lukewarm water, I turn back. Downhill on the wide ski slope is banging rather than running. Such steep descents are not a Belgian Ardennes offensive. After a few bends, I dive into a random forest path. Everything downwards is good. I'll find Chamonix somehow. During a hit by Red Zebra I pull out one of the mp3 earphones. A path full of loose stones and branches at full tilt is best read with feet and ears together.

I can't piss in the toilet
Can't sleep in my bedroom
There's no food in the kitchen
I can't live in a living room.

SEARCH & RESCUE

Half an hour or so later I'm back at my starting point. My upper legs are completely soured. No pain in my shins, knee or heel. I take off my shoes and dip my legs in the ice-cold water of the fountain near the church. I pry myself out of my running backpack and fish for coins for a can of soft drink.

Soon I hit myself on the head. The zipper of the race vest containing my energy gels is still open. My smartphone, which I'd stuffed into the same compartment, is gone.

I look upward, hopelessly.

The thing is several years old and can't be localized by GPS. It's full of pictures and contacts I don't keep in any cloud - I'm too analog for that. And retracing my steps is out of the question. 24 hours later, after unsuccessful inquiries at the tourist office and the police station, I do. My search & rescue mission yields nothing more than a meeting with a mountain buck. The cry with which he warns his fellows of my arrival is halfway between the sound of vomiting and the German metal band Rammstein.

I buy a prepaid mobile in a newsagent's. Again back to the police station. Then along to the tourist office, where I inform my family and loved ones by e-mail that for the time being I can be reached only on a French mobile phone number. Again, both searches prove fruitless.

Disconsolately I start on the 5 km return journey from Chamonix to my campsite in Les Bossons. The temperature drops quickly, which is no gift in sweaty running clothes. No sense in waiting for a bus. I urge my stiff legs to set to again, with the compromise that I stick my thumb out with every approaching car.

PLANET OF THE APES

I cross the street at Lac des Gaillands. A campfire in the forest attracts my attention. I'm halfway, but nobody has given me a lift. Warm up for a minute? Soon not only the smoke from the campfire but also the smell of marijuana wafts towards me.

I realize that for them I'm turning up out of nowhere. I carefully shuffle closer and signal my presence with my head lamp.

"Mais oui! Bienvenu! Welcome! Fwieeeeeeeeeeeet!"

My host looks like a clown without makeup and farts into a golden-yellow trumpet. I hunker down between the empty wine cartons and stretch my hands out to the fire. Apart from me, a few washed-out forest elves with dreadlocks. A man with a wide skaters' pullover gives me his hand. He apologizes that he can no longer offer me a glass. A lift to the campsite, that he can offer soon.

I lie on my side to absorb as much heat as possible from the fire. The unpainted clown has now exchanged his trumpet for two burning fire-breathing torches. He surges through the pine trees with them like a fire spirit that has just jacked up. His arms and legs make long shadows that skim along the tops of the pines. His *danse macabre* takes my eyes to two snow-white glacier tongues that crawl out of the Mont Blanc massif to the valley. About it a cloudless starry sky that maybe makes the decor look even bigger than during the day.

In 1966, the pilot of Air India Flight 101 thought that you could steadily descend once past Mont Blanc. On the way from Bombay to London, with a planned stopover in Geneva, the plane with the name Kanchenjunga, however, ended up on a rock between the two glaciers. No fewer than 117 passengers lost their lives. There were also fifteen Indian monkeys on board. In my imagination, these animals, intended for English test labs, survived the crash and built a secret colony under the ice of the Glacier des Bossons and Glacier des Taconnaz for the past half century.

Forget about the cosmos. *Planet of the Apes* is in Chamonix.

Trumpetman gives a cry behind me. Stumbled over his own feet. With his butt up between the pine needles. A flesh-shaped pyramid.

Wouldn't the monkeys laugh themselves crooked at so much clumsiness?

TUUT-TUUT

A text message on my French mobile phone.

"Rik, a mountain guide found your smartphone and sent me a reply from your inbox. You can pick it up at the Bureau des Guides du Mont Blanc."

Tarts' luck, they'd have said in my village. ▲▲▲

Nepal
MUSTANG MOUNTAIN TRAIL RACE

Not a competition, but a privilege

Nepal
MUSTANG MOUNTAIN TRAIL RACE

166KM | 100MI • 8 STAGES
D+ 8,200M | 26,903FT

- Geological mecca
- Spiritual
- Short stages make altitude & distance digestible

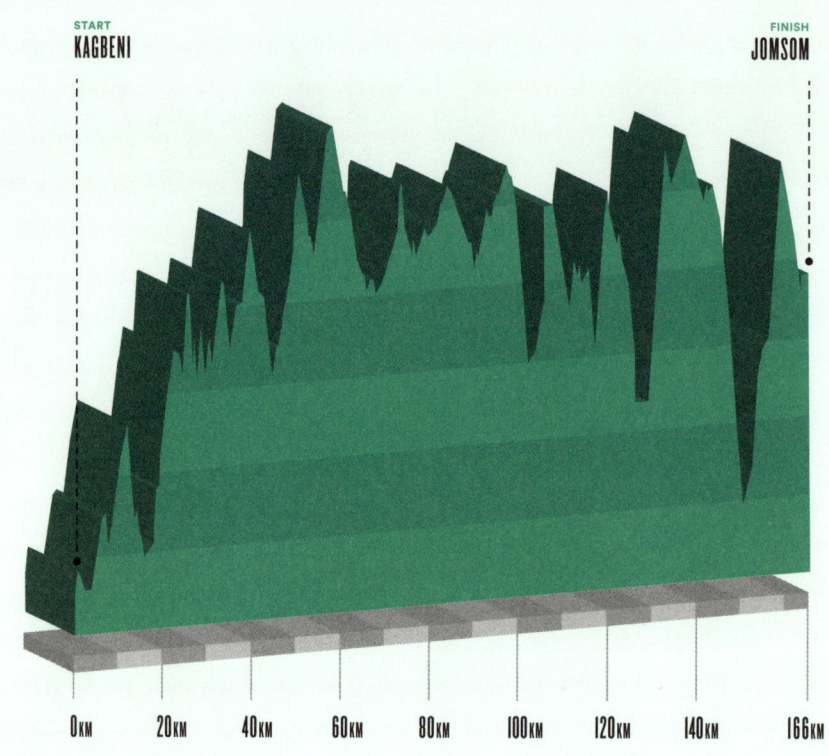

START
KAGBENI

FINISH
JOMSOM

0KM   20KM   40KM   60KM   80KM   100KM   120KM   140KM   166KM

ERICA RUSBRIDGE

Age 53 • Project coordinator
Perth • Australia

Why did you choose this race?

ERICA "Every two years, I take part in a big race abroad. I'd been to Bhutan once before and had lost my heart to the Himalayas, so it was only a matter of time before I went to Nepal. I already knew of the Everest Trail Race®, but then I bumped into a promo movie of the Mustang Mountain Trail Race online. I knew immediately I'd found what I was looking for. I now work as a project coordinator for the government, but in the past, I was a metal scientist working in the mining industry. Let's say that I have a particular love for geological peculiarities. It was in my former work in the Goldfields that I'd seen such wide and dramatic landscapes. Nowhere else in the world do you find a red rock desert with such grand canyons, while at the same time you are face-to-face with snowy 8,000-metre peaks like Annapurna and Dhaulagiri. There is also another, more trivial reason. There are also races in Europe that interest me, but Nepal is just that bit closer" (laughs).

How did you prepare?

ERICA "I used to do triathlons. In the Ironman competitions, I realized that I was made for the longer work. I'm a diesel engine: never fast, but I finish the job. This made ultras the logical next step. However, I must add that where I live it's not easy to train for a mountain race. It's rather flat. The nearest mountain of any consequence, Bluff Knoll in the Stirling Range, is 400 kilometres away: 1,099 metres high with 650 metres' climbing. You can grind the miles with long runs, but climbing requires something else from your body. That's why I also conclude every training period for an important race with a weekend on Bluff Knoll, to dot the i's. Not that I'm out for a fast finishing time in competitions. For me, training for this type of race is simply an excuse to take time for myself. When I sign up for an ultra, it's always like giving myself permission to find a goal in the challenge that doesn't quite scare me off. It's in that focus that I find peace. Fortunately, my husband and my two children support me. They know that it instils new life into me. And they are also part of the story as support crew and cheerers."

How did your race go?

ERICA "The scale of the landscape you spend a whole week in is incredible. Put simply, you run from 2,900 to 4,300 metres altitude. From the start to the end of the valley and back again.

Race secret

In Konchok Ling, the race director interrupts the race for a tourist outing. You climb along a rope up to a natural rock dwelling full of ancient Buddhist murals. The upper part of the valley has thousands of such sky caves. In prehistoric times, these dwellings served as safe accommodation. Later, with the arrival of Buddhism, they were given a religious function. Nowadays, an occasional snow leopard chooses such a hollow as a lair. So no beef jerky in your running backpack, please.

The stages are easy to do, with distances between 15 and 30 kilometres, but the altitude really does make itself felt. Fortunately, the race schedule also gives time for acclimatization. This is an incredibly desolate area. You cross small villages of a dozen households, but never more. Formerly the valley was a kingdom of its own where foreigners were not welcome, but nowadays it belongs to Nepal. You notice that it has very much its own identity. Not only because of the remote and isolated nature of the region, but also because of the influence of the Tibetan language and culture. Away from the impact of modernity, this valley's inhabitants appear to have developed a way of life that must have been the same for thousands of years. Simply because modernity contributes little or nothing to their existence. I was there as a tourist, a visitor from that modernity. You are welcome, but you remain a passer-by. I see this race

therefore as a privilege rather than a pure race. You come for the experience, not for a personal record. I was fortunate that three geologists also ran in the year I took part. Better company for such a unique environment I could not wish for."

Which moment will you never forget?

ERICA "During the race, I heard an explosion in the distance. A dull bang and then the splitting of rocks. I guessed what it was, because I recognize that sound from a thousand owing to my experience in mining. I asked the *race director* and he confirmed my suspicion. The thunder came from the Chinese, who were constructing a road ahead. Such a sad moment. One that also made me so angry. Such a road serves primarily the trade interests of the Chinese. Why else would they build it? But it can certainly also be an opportunity. Many families currently send their children to Kathmandu to study and work there. Ah, it's a difficult balance to get right. The Nepalese government guards the region's individuality, charging each tourist 50 US dollars a day for a 'permit'. Not that it stops hikers. The region is simply too beautiful, but that money goes directly into the local economy. I wonder if the Chinese will have the same concern for this region's vulnerability."

A golden tip for future participants?

ERICA "Your pores are wide open owing to the altitude. You just evaporate where you stand. That is why it's very important to drink a lot and often, because otherwise you totally dehydrate. As an Australian, I often train at temperatures of 40°C. The habit of hydrating well is in my DNA. In addition, I would also recommend altitude sickness pills. I didn't need them, but it seems better to have them. And lots of sunscreen."

"There are moments when you feel like wild horses couldn't stop you."

Lizzy Hawker

SHEPHERD

I'll laugh until my head comes off
Women and children first
And children first
And children

Here I'm alive
Everything all of the time
Here I'm alive
Everything all of th…

After three hours, my mp3 player's battery dies on me. To keep my mind occupied, I let my imagination run free. Kilian Jornet lives a few villages away from here in an old water mill. Not impossible that our tracks will cross.

FANTASY

What would it be like to train here with him now?

"*Hola*, Kilian!"
"Ah, Rikkieboy! *Com estàs?*"
"*Ça va, jong.* Glad it's a bit fresher, such a hot day."
"Ja, hé …"
"Done anything special today?"

"Buf, an early morning run up and down Mont Blanc. This afternoon I had to cut our Emelie's grass. And to finish the day, a short evening run over the Col des Posettes. Enfin, next year I want to go to the Himalayas for Mount Everest. So yes, keep training,…"
"Up and down Mont Blanc again. You crazy fucker! How did it go?"
"*Same same, but different.* Far too many people. They all know my face too. Annoying! An autograph here, a selfie there. And that queuing on those mountain ridges. I can't train properly like that. I want to be alone with my mountains."
"*I see …*"

If Kilian weren't a sponsored champion, I'm almost certain he'd be a shepherd in the high Pyrenees - in close contact with the seasons and nature. Lonely and misunderstood, but also hospitable and generous to passers-by with a warm heart.

A twist in my train of thought takes me to a crazy story that I once saw on YouTube. Cliff Young, a 61-year-old Australian shepherd, appeared in 1983 in rubber boots and workwear at the start of the 850 km

Sydney-Melbourne race. Concerned, the other participants asked if he knew what he was letting himself in for. After all, a six-day trail run is no pony camp. His answer was clear:

"I'm a shepherd. I've neither tractor nor horse. When the weather's bad, I have to go after my animals and hunt them in. And then sometimes I run for more than 24 hours at a time. Yes, I think I can do this. I was able to take some vacation right now. So here I am!"

Cliff had never run such a race before. Did he know that the other athletes run for 18 hours and sleep 6? The first night he just went on. And didn't stop on subsequent nights. Despite his slow shuffle, which became known as the *Cliff Young Shuffle*, he won the race with a 12-hour improvement in the course record.

THE LADIES' MONT BLANC

"Kiki, a little slower. You're going too fast for me!" I burble breathlessly.

"OK, ça va ... Say, did I tell you I'm moving to Norway with Emelie?"

"Fantastic! Kilian, honest ... Aren't you a bit sick by now of all this training? Aren't there times when you wonder why you're doing all this?"

"Gosh, no. Nobody forces me to do this. I started running in the mountains to maintain my winter sports condition over the summer. Actually, I don't see myself as a runner. Rather as someone who likes to move in the mountains. Maybe I just need this to feel that I'm alive? Except…"

"Yes?"

"Except when death gets involved. A few years ago, my climbing partner had a fatal accident at my side. That cut me up badly. But it's part of it. We all know that

mountains can be cruel, but the passion is just stronger. Then you accept that risk without defying fate."

"Say, Kilian, two days ago I did Mont Buet. Up to 3,096 metres, without crampons, on my trail shoes. 1,700 metres up and down. *Light and fast*, like you. It was blissful!"

"Haha! Allez, Rik ... Don't blind-copy me. We've different safety margins with the difference in talent and experience. Of course we always have to be careful in the mountains, but on Mont Buet you still had a lot of leeway, you know."

"How so?"

"Kilian Jornet lives a few villages away from here in an old watermill. Not impossible that our tracks will cross."

"That mountain is nicknamed *Mont Blanc des Dames*! Haha!"

Kilian spurts away in a flash. He chooses a different path, while I continue the descent to Le Tour. I switch my headlamp to the brightest position, and the light beam detects my breathing and streaks of fog.

"For a long time already, I've been running, not against the mountains, but with them."

HARDWARE TEST

Without music and Kilian, it's all of a sudden deafeningly silent. It's like a sacred sound interrupted only by the grinding of my trail shoes on the gravel path. For a long time already, I've been running, not against the mountains, but with them. It was hard work getting here, but I don't get much

sensation from it. This moment has nothing to do with ego. Not even with emotions. What I experience comes from deeper. I'm present in a special and timeless way.

This is where my strength is.

My sports watch says nearly midnight when I turn off my headlamp and enter the *Micro-Brasserie de Chamonix*. The bar caught my attention on my way here. On the way I marked the establishment as the unofficial finishing line of my hardware test for my upcoming ultra-marathon. I clock off at 35 kilometres, 2,000 metres up and 2,000 metres down in 5 hours.

I finally feel a real trail runner again. Mr Beer-Belly is no more.

"Eat this, bro." "Go fuck yourself!"
   Can Salomon come and make a short documentary about my well-trained body?

The menu I find on the counter shows home-made spare ribs as the special promotion, setting off a Pavlovian reaction in my mouth. There's still a light in the kitchen. Are the stoves still on? If not, do I have enough appetite to force down some leftovers heated in the microwave? Preferably, a surplus of those home-made spare ribs, because in my head the fat is already dripping from my hands, lips and beard.

BEER

The waiter shakes his head. The kitchen's been closed for half an hour. Everything's cleaned and washed away. The cook's hanging on the corner of the counter above a glass of brown rum. This man's not moving anymore tonight. The only thing the waiter can provide is salted peanuts. I ask with a straight face if I can get a plate full of them, because my body needs fuel. His smile as a reaction is disarming. I immediately order half a litre of locally produced artisan beer. I hesitate for a moment, but after nine weeks without a drop of alcohol it seems a fair deal.

A few handfuls of salted peanuts and half a glass of beer later, the first signs of sedation appear. I stare at the dancing bodies in the hellish disco light belonging to a local cover band. The front rows roar the utopian chorus of Red Hot Chili Peppers:

First born unicorn
Hard core soft porn
Dream of Californication
Dream of Californication

The funky guitar playing promises a night full of excitement. Yet I feel very lonely. In addition to a shot of Kilian Jornet, I also bear a piece of Anthony Kiedis in me. It's not creatives that live in the mountains, but workers. Stonemasons, cheesemakers and herb-growers and gatherers. Down-to-earth people, people with moderation. Everything that the singer of the Red Hot Chili Peppers is not. I know it too: greedily playing hero and afterwards crawling home with your demons. Would his career have been different if he had had the Mont Blanc massif instead of all kinds of drugs as a plaything?

What if I become a shepherd?

Or a hermit?

Do the Japanese 'Marathon Monks' at the monastery of Mount Hiei still have vacancies? ▲▲▲

France

FESTIVAL DES TEMPLIERS

13 TRAIL RACES • 1 WEEKEND

"I don't know about you, but the thought of downing Roquefort cheese at an aid station in the middle of a challenging trail ultramarathon just isn't all that alluring."

Adam W. Chase
RUNNER'S WORLD

PARTY

"Hey, shit..." "Rik, what's happening? Don't move!"
Unlike his wife, Jean-Charles remains stoical under the thick line of blood that drips from my index finger onto my palm. Christiane was serving her homemade dry sausage as an extra to the spaghetti. I was so busy chatting with my Swiss host family that I didn't notice that I'd cut off a piece of my finger along with the slice of sausage. The mother of the house jumps up and rushes to the medicine cabinet. She pulls my hand to the tap, rinses away the blood and works exuberantly with disinfectant, gauze and tape.

I'm not even at the starting line and already have an injury.

At 10 o'clock in the lower part of the valley, the starting signal will be given for the race for which I've prepared during a whole spring and summer. I offer to help with the dishes, but my Swiss mother-for-one-night is resolute.

"Bed time, *jeune homme*."

She'd shown me her grandchildren's spare room upon arrival. A old pine double bed as a resting place. A plastic child's bed as a counter for my race clothing and equipment. My running shoes neatly at the door. The window open a crack.

Ready.

Although the familiar smell of neighbouring pines and the eternal mountain silence have calmed me, it's difficult to sink into a deep sleep. I'm not really nervous about the race. Ultimately I'll be doing tomorrow what I've been doing for the whole summer. Unconsciously, of course, the tension is simmering. Bored, I turn on the night light, crawl out of bed and shuffle as quietly as possible to the bookcase. The German-language children's book on trolls brings no solace, just the hope that these freaks will not be standing next to me on the starting line tomorrow.

A text message wakes me before my alarm clock. The brother of my now-dead childhood friend is usually parsimonious with loaded messages, but on high days like this he's always on his toes:

His text message doesn't surprise me. Just like his late brother, he loves the mountains. As a thirteen-year-old he stood with him, his sister and his father at the summit of Mont Blanc. A trick he repeated a few years ago with friends. Was I envious? I almost ate up my mountain shoes. Besides the love of mountains, our shared mourning has bound us for life. Obviously we don't talk about that often, because real men don't talk about their emotions.

I answer briefly and turn onto my side. My body's not awake yet. In my head, I run through my entire mission. Failure is a human right, but not today. The effort is clear. Two years ago I was here for the Marathon du Mont-Blanc. At that time, I was hardly a trail runner. Today I want to really go all out, without blowing myself up like I did then. Reading the mountains out loud, like a record player needle in the single track of a vinyl record. For a majestic story with high notes and deep basses you have to go up and down.

"I was so busy chatting with my Swiss host family that I didn't notice that I'd cut off a piece of my finger along with the slice of sausage."

THE MENU?

The OCC - an acronym for the 56 kilometres of mountain paths between Orsières, Champex and Chamonix. From Switzerland to France, with 3,500 metres vertical climb. This race counts as the equivalent of a 90-kilometre flat race.

Standing here at the starting line is a privilege in itself. To register you have to collect points by completing other similar races. Luck also plays a part, as you are certain of a starting ticket only after a draw. What the Iron Man in Hawaii is for triathlon, this mediagenic meeting in Chamonix is for trail running. If it's your sport, you must have done it once - the Ultra-Trail du Mont-Blanc®. Another abbreviation: the UTMB®.

I confess, I'm not targeting the main bird. The OCC is - in addition to the CCC, TDS and PTL - the shortest variant of this Abbreviation Paradise. The actual original root race is the UTMB® itself. This race takes runners 170 kilometres around the Mont Blanc massif. An experienced walker with heavy luggage easily takes seven days to complete this route with more than 10,000 vertical metres of climbing.

As a trail runner, you have up to 46 hours and 30 minutes to complete this tour. 42.23% of the participants in this year's edition will give up. Only 30.76% of the participants will reach the finish in Chamonix in time.

"Maybe those UTMB® runners are less crazy than they seem?"

I'm running just a third of that distance. Which lunatics choose the complete package? Every year around 2,300 runners are under starter's orders. Often environmentally-conscious, middle-aged, middle-class men - that's what the statistics teach us. But surely, isn't a 10 km jog enough for a shot of endorphins in full mid-life crisis? *The mountains are calling and I must go?* The shine of UTMB®-FINISHER on your Facebook wall? How many marriages have already been killed by this training-intensive quest?

"Curiosity can be a real bastard," says American North Face® trail runner and UTMB® finisher Timothy Olson. "You have no control over it. You just have to go through with it. This competition makes you humble, because there's no guarantee of success. But you can try."

As a leisure activity, healthier, in any case, than the lines of coke he snorted in his previous life.

"There have been dark moments in my life when I didn't know exactly what I wanted to do. I was heavily into drugs. I realized I had a problem when I needed cocaine to just get out of bed in the morning. I didn't want to continue like this. I wanted to get all of this out of my life. Trail running turned out to be my lifebuoy."

Climbing and descending for hours in response to an unconscious cry for *rewilding* and meaning. Maybe those UTMB® runners are less crazy than they seem?

START

Christiane pushes me forward. "You've not left anything in your room?" she asks me as she closes her front door and I step into her car. There's not much to forget. My luggage is still in Chamonix. I arrived here yesterday in a race outfit with my running backpack containing the mandatory survival items for the race. And a plastic bag full of empty packets of pre-race carbohydrates, which I washed down yesterday on the train from Chamonix to Martigny. My fellow passengers watched my feast wide-eyed. The mountains of sugar waffles, granola bars, crisps and dates were at least as imposing as the landscape we were passing through.

You don't just do an ultra-run. You build up a basis over months or years. You maintain your body like a perfectionist gardener who pulls every weed. No leaf too many, no blade of grass too long. And on the race day, you kick everything up brutally with your garden boots. The result is supposedly called satisfaction. With 5 minutes to the starting gun, I'm not that sure anymore. Actually, I would have preferred to have stayed cosily with Jean-Charles and Christiane, but I've not travelled here to help harvest sauerkraut from their garden.

I wanna run, I want to hide
I wanna tear down the walls
That hold me inside
I wanna reach out
And touch the flame
Where the streets have no name.

The U2 anthem echoes through the Rue de l'Eglise. Race director Catherine Poletti is duty MC. With the build of a sturdy hut guard, she looks the antithesis of the 1,414 trained runners on this starting line. As if it was a fairground race round the church tower, she counts and gives the starting shot. I shake myself through a tunnel of toddlers and school children for whom lessons start only after we've passed. Dozens of high fives at knee height are a logical consequence. At Som la Proz, the largest cow bells seem to have been brought out from the barn. Their drone makes my body shake.

The bubble of a race gives me a structure to exist in. Follow the signalling ribbons straight ahead over Bovine, Catogne and La Flégère. Three sturdy cols up and down, with the mathematical certainty that the discomfort ends at the finish. A primitive mission with no complex layering. I blast ahead - in contrast to real life, where choices sometimes paralyse me like a worm. To the left or right? Do I opt for that job or do I go into that vacancy? What do my head, my gut and my heart tell me? And what do I choose if they contradict each other? To choose is also to lose. It often seems like I want to save myself that pain. I realize that you can only evaluate a choice after you have experienced the result. You get on a train. In a coming station you can change trains if you want. But you first and foremost have to get onto that train, because staying on the platform makes no sense. More than once I've caught myself knowing all the lines, destinations and departure times by heart, but wandering discontented with a cold coffee on the platforms until all the trains have left. Not choosing can be a strategy to avoid the tensions inherent in a choice or connection. Have I still not yet learned to handle these tensions?

"Mountaineering is adventure. And adventure involves risk by definition. I started my career as a rock climber. Difficult routes require focus. Not a little, but your full attention. I've continued this lesson into my life. When I climb, I climb. When I write, I write. When I'm with my family, my head is also with my family. When I give a lecture, the lecture is the only thing I'm doing at the time. Fragmenting your attention is, in my opinion, not very satisfying or efficient", I would hear legendary Italian mountaineer Reinhold Messner say a few months later at a lecture.

MANTRA

On the climb up to Bovine, the OCC shows its teeth for the first time. The sun is approaching its highest point of the day and tells me mercilessly that I need to take her into account. Just before the summit I have to stand in the shade to lower my body temperature. Did I start too fast?

How hot could it be?

35°C or more?

During the first descent I think back to an interview with the Nepalese Dawa Sherpa, who won the first UTMB® in 2003. In retrospect, he had to admit that he never trained. During the week he worked as a construction worker. The 20 kilometres to and from his work he did by bicycle. On weekends he took part in mountain races. If Dawa Sherpa could win the UTMB® in this way, then my 35 kilometres to and from school and 4 weeks of mountain holidays should still save me for the much shorter OCC.

"Anthropologist John Kennedy reports that the average Tarahumara spends at least one hundred days a year heavily drunk on or hungover from their homebrewed corn beer."

At the aid station in Trient, I fill up with ice-cold cola, salty biscuits and an energy gel. Quickly duck my head under the garden hose and then head back 1,000 metres vertical. Risk is management. During my stay in Chamonix I saw my time on the vertical kilometre rise to 1 hour and 10 minutes. I was told that this is the toughest climb of the race. I give myself some extra time and set 1 hour and 20 minutes as my target to the top of Catogne.

I remember that my mantra smells like *Born to Run*. Like in the chapter in which Christopher McDougall describes the legendary battle between track record holder Ann Trason and some Tarahumara on the Leadville Trail 100 in Colorado in the 1990s. The rational, competitive West versus a bunch of primitives in sandals. While the other runners had pain in their faces, the Tarahumara looked a bunch of exuberant dogs on ecstasy. The world's sports press was there watching. McDougall names minimal footwear and chia seeds as the outer shell of their running secret. The Tarahumara get their real strength from the pleasure that is part of their running. Fun, compassion and gratitude as the ultimate doping? Sounds distinctly tree-hugging.

Columnist George Beinhorn is resolute. He finds McDougall's portrait of the Tarahumara particularly idealized. Anthropologist John Kennedy reports that the average Tarahumara spends at least one hundred days a year heavily drunk on or hung over from their home-brewed corn beer. In this context, Beinhorn also talks about nocturnal bacchanals in which social tensions find an outlet in bloody fistfights and extramarital sex parties.

Tree-hugging?

My ass… ▲▲▲

Morocco
MARATHON
DES
SABLES

239.3KM | 149.1MI • D+ 3,500M | 11,482FT

"I constantly asked myself if I was enjoying this, the heat, the hills, the sand, the thirst, the hunger, and basically the answer is NO, I didn't enjoy it as such but the adventure was more than memorable."

Nick Butter

WWW.NICKBUTTERRUNNING.COM

WOLF

At the Franco-Swiss summit in Catogne, a volunteer scans my race bib. A bottle of lukewarm water is pressed into my hand. The col I most feared is now behind me. The next step is to reduce altitude by 795 vertical metres over a distance of 6 kilometres. Half the race is behind me and I begin to smell home. Time to take out my secret weapon again. So far I've used my mp3 player for only a few minutes. The grooves pumped me up too much on the climb. In combination with the heat, my engine would have exploded. But for an elongated descent it's just fine. This isn't trail running, but dancing. I press play and hit Dave Grohl.

Run and tell all of the angels
This could take all night
Think I need a devil to help me get things right.

Seven curves, thirteen tree roots, eighteen boulders and thirty pine cones later, I lie flat on my stomach. The dust and dry pine needles stick to my sweaty forearms. Because of the music I was too much in my head and I failed to spot that fourteenth tree root in time. With all the consequences. Meanwhile, the Foo Fighters continued to do their thing.

Fly along with me
I can't quite make it alone
Try to make this life my own
Fly along with me
I can't quite make it alone
Try to make this life my own.

Little did I know in those silent seconds as my courage drained out of me that, two weeks later, the same guys would release a song with the title 'Run' on their tenth studio album.

Wake up
Run for your life with me
Wake up
Run for your life with me.

I scan my body. No headache, I can see OK. Wrists not broken. I pull myself up. No blood on my shirt. I cling to a tilting fir tree and stretch my cramped right calf. Blood on the left knee, but I don't see any wound for which a doctor would take needle and thread out of his cabinet.

"Hey, are you OK?"

Like on my Marathon du Mont-Blanc, when I went into the forest to relieve myself, competitors who keep an eye on things are a kind of life insurance policy. If I'm to believe ultra-phenomenon Scott Jurek, his fellow runners are even more than that:

"Why I take part in races is not to beat the others, but to be together with them. Some runners try to handle the pain by imagining the audience of an Olympic stadium shouting them on. Others use music as a distraction. I have another trick. I focus on others, because it's easy to get outside of yourself when you're thinking about someone else."

Does that ring a bell?

The traditional running of the Tarahumara is all about teamwork. A community that celebrates itself and honours individual members.

Same same, but different?
Not really so tree-hugging after all?
"Yeah, man. All good! Let's go ...."
It takes a few more turns before I've shaken the stiffness out of my muscles. I decide to leave that mp3 player for what it is. Gradually the self-confidence comes back and I dare to speed up a bit.

'THIS IS YOUR PARTY!'

Where the forest turns into meadow, the first spectators pop up along the path. A long tunnel of clapping, supportive eye contact and encouraging words in a variety of languages as far as the aid station in Vallorcine. Unconsciously I straighten my back for so many spectators. Not for long, for a few seconds after my arrival I hang bent in two over an aluminium wash basin. The cold water runs over my neck.

VERY HOT

Really it's far too hot for physical efforts. A thoughtful person would spend an afternoon like this dressed in a djellaba in an establishment with piles of dates and litres of sweet tea within reach - preferably under a set of fans that spread the fragrant smoke of the apple tobacco from antique water pipes.

"Seven curves, thirteen tree roots, eighteen boulders and thirty pinecones later, I lie flat on my stomach."

I take off my running backpack. I'd really love to sit staring in front of myself for half an hour, but the clock is ticking and brings me back to reality. I open a zipper to see what's left of my rations. From the range of bags and flasks I take one energy gel with a triple dose of caffeine. Eventually I add a chocolate-flavoured power bar. And a tablet with a set of concentrated essential amino acids, which I flush with ice-cold cola.

After filling up with water, I hit the road again. First walking, to get my body moving again. After a few minutes, as the caffeine kicks in, I speed up into a jogging-like rhythm. Immediately I also understand why the word 'jogging' has the Middle English *schogge* (to shake/jerk) as its etymological root. Despite the psychological advantage of knowing this valley like the back of my hand from my training sessions, the climb to Col des Montets is a messy one. A short descent later the route shoots upwards from Argentière one last time. Before the start, this 610-metre vertical climb to La Flégère seemed like a piece of cake. I reconnoitred the climb a month ago. What was then a leisurely training session now feels like a queue of suffering souls. Wanting to go faster, but being unable to. Occasionally I exchange looks with another runner. They too are in the death zone. Our conversations, wordless, are revealing.

'We are warriors of the same tribe' their eyes tell me.

PALE ALE

I pull myself up on my running sticks. A few minutes ago I drank the last drops of my water supply. The puddle that I just made smelled anything but fresh and looked like a glass of Indian Pale Ale. Strange, because I already had 6 litres of water inside me. It's only 3 kilometres to the next and last aid station, but it seems to me, no matter how ridiculous, not feasible without a bridging loan. Maybe all that struggling is not so noble?

"Which wolves are going to celebrate their arrival tonight with chronic diarrhoea?"

'It's liberating to flirt with madness. Once people cross their borders, they cross them a long way', says a sociologist in a newspaper article about binge drinking at winter sports après-ski parties.

Does his theory also apply to this alcohol-free summer sport?

A few turns later the path turns the corner. The scene in front of me tells me I wasn't the only one with uncontrollable coercion. A dozen runners are quenching their thirst at a mountain stream. Some lie with their heads fully submerged in the ice-cold water. Others take a shower to cool off. Again those tacit we-understand-each-other looks. Society is far away here.

The scene reminds me of the 'caveman approach' of Anton Krupicka, an iconic American distance runner who likes to keep everything minimal except for his hair and beard. He prefers to train bare-chested, unimpeded by energy gels, drinking bottles or water bag. In extreme need you can always find water at the foot of some glacier. Can it be more romantic?

TRANSBOUNDARY

"It just sucks to carry shit... And this way you teach your body to live on less. In a race I eat and drink as I should. Because of that fuel my races often feel lighter than my training sessions. That gives wings!" he says.

I squat down, immerse the scarf I'm wearing on my head and cool my face. I look around and suddenly I know. Can it be denied? Man is and remains an animal. A set of primates! Or not... A pack of wolves, that's us! Possibly not with the same intestines. This melt water has already travelled a long way. No idea how many cows and mountain goats have already done their business here. Which wolves are going to celebrate their arrival tonight with chronic diarrhoea?

Finishing an ultra-trail is like crossing a border. In a certain sense, it's just that. I once read an interview by Emelie Forsberg. She noted that excessive drinking, overwork and overeating are also forms of systematically crossing boundaries. In contrast to running, this last enumeration can be linked to many modern-day ailments such as stress, burnout and obesity. Long distances in nature confront you with what you really need and how little that actually is.

"We often make it more complicated than it is with treatments, diets, mindfulness and all kinds of attempts to keep ourselves going. I think that the answers and solutions for this kind of thing do not have to be sought outside ourselves, but always lie within and reveal themselves as soon as we are willing to listen."

Emelie Forsberg, the blonde she-wolf from the Far North?

The La Flégère aid station announces the end of a climb that followed an exposed ski slope for the last vertical metres. I let myself be served by the volunteers who ask me what I need. Just 825 vertical metres *downhill* to the finish in Chamonix.

M'AS-TU VU? TOWEL

This'll be no problem, I realize. And faster than I thought. A few months ago I watched an OCC report by a Dutchman who looked pretty well-trained. He had done the route in 12 hours and 30 minutes. An end-time that seemed too crazy for words to me. The idea of arriving before sunset carries me down the forest slope.

The first asphalt I encounter feels like a smooth highway. I check my watch. It's almost 6:30 pm. The heat of this afternoon is in its death throes. With a plate of pasta and a half a litre of coke inside me, I could see myself running into the cooler night. My tank had a hard time with the high temperatures, but isn't yet completely empty. I'm glad that I'm coming close to the finishing line and am not yet in my grave.

The crush barriers tell me I've reached Rue Joseph Vallot. After hours spent strung out in nature, this last part is a brutal shock. Just like with the Marathon du Mont-Blanc. Again too many people, too much concrete. Too many shops selling irrelevant souvenirs. As if you wake up on the train from a beneficent nap, and suddenly realize that you're naked in the compartment and everyone's staring at you.

But they are metres I know I will never forget, even though I still have my clothes on. Applause, for the first to the last participant. Hands that press an ice cream, coffee or beer into every passing runner's hands. I pull out my earphones in order to be as present as possible. Even so, Millionaire doesn't give up. The band plays on in my back pocket without an audience.

I'm on a high and I can't stop rolling
My heart is open, yeah, I'm doing it solo
I'm on a high and this is my time, our time
I'm on a high and I can't stop rolling.

A last turn to Place de l'Eglise.

That iconic finishing arch.

So…

With 9 hours and 29 minutes, I'm 259th of 1,231 finishers.

That was it.

'All kinds of feelings of abandonment can creep into our lives and make us doubt our right to exist. Unconsciously the tendency can arise to have to prove ourselves constantly as if to justify our existence. In this way lots of energy can be spent in producing great performances over and over again. Eventually this will lead to exhaustion, because it fails to give the satisfaction we really seek. The more we do our best, the more we deny that we are allowed to be as we are. It's better to look these emotions straight in the eye and embrace them', I will read later in a lifestyle magazine.

After the finish I disentangle myself from my soaking wet running backpack. In my hands a far too warm OCC FINISHER jacket. I'm proud of the *m'as-tu-vu?* jacket I've just earned, but currently the garment is useless. I continue to strip to my running shorts and shuffle to the fire hose hanging from the church fence. Only once the heavy water crashes onto my shoulder blades do I realize what I've done.

I dry myself with my *m'as-tu-vu?* towel

I want to send my parents a message that I've arrived safe and sound. I've hardly pulled my smartphone out of my backpack and it starts ringing. My father was following the race online and saw that I'd arrived.

"On to the next!" he toasts.

A few hours later I also have my mother on the line. On events like this, it remains strange to hear them separately.

"Remember this moment, Rik!" she says.

In my head I've already chosen an 80-kilometre race in six months' time.

And now let's go looking for a postcard with a glorious Mont Blanc for Mr Beer-Belly. ▲▲▲

"The idea of arriving before sunset carries me down the forest slope."

South Africa
OTTER AFRICAN TRAIL RUN

42κμ | 26.1ΜΙ • D+ 2,600μ | 8,530ΓΤ

"After the beach section we hit the Otter in full brute force, facing the first set of numerous sets of stairs straight out of hell. In my life I have never experienced so much cursing during a race."

Riana Scholtz
WWW.TOUCHANDGO.COM

TITLE

The washing-up water gurgles out of the sink. Finally done. I throw the stale dishcloth onto the rack, take a cup of coffee and shuffle to my laptop. Out of the speakers comes Body Count, the hip hop metal ensemble around American grand master Ice-*mothafuckin'*-T.

Of course I scream along. I've known the entire album off by heart since my teens. The band already accompanied me several times on training runs and even then I couldn't prevent myself getting more into their music. Crossing a forest and singing aloud, I don't hurt anyone. At most I chase away the fauna with my roar. It becomes problematic only when you cross other forest visitors and burden them with this not-in-polite-society language.

I sit down and write the last sentences of a sixth chapter of this book.

EX-RUNNER

It summarizes my story. From runner to non-runner. Again runner, then trail runner. Then again nothing. And again something. And again.

A pro-running story with anti-running as a mountainous red thread.

Jesus, Rik, why always so bloody pompous? Precisely an overdose of post-modernism. Be more playful! I erase 'mountainous', and immediately after that 'pro-running' and 'anti-running'. No one will understand that. Too academic for a baseline too. And certainly for a subtitle.

'Ex-runner' eventually finds its way into the recycle bin. It covers anything but the cargo. And it sounds too much like Herman Brusselmans' *Ex-lover* and *Ex-drummer*. We may be from the same city, but that's where the likeness stops.

I'm too much in my head again.

This damned contemplativeness.

What am I doing? Isn't it easier to not look back? More than likely, but I can't help it. I've started to write and new sentences are constantly popping up in my mind. I present myself, Mr Beer-Belly and my earlier incarnations as spectators of my own intimacy.

Now that sounded like it came straight out of a church magazine.

Are other trail runners actually asking for this personal story? I'm not Haruki Murakami, the Japanese novelist-runner of the celebrated *What I talk about when I talk about running*.

MAYBE I SHOULD JUST KEEP MY MOUTH SHUT?

Or write just for myself?

Body and soul are interlinked. My running story is therefore also a story of my thinking. I cannot tell it any other way. If it's in you like that, it has to come out. For some people this may seem like redundant narcissistic waffling. Readers who don't care for my personal thoughts can always skip a few paragraphs or go for a run.

I know that many long-distance runners carry stories in their backpacks, stories which dance prettily or bounce about as they run.

Disconnect in order to connect better.

Writing about yourself isn't always pleasant, I've noticed in the meantime. It's not always easy to be human towards oneself. With me, self-reflection quickly turns to exaggerated self-preoccupation, isolation and loneliness. One of the healthiest things a person can do is stay away from it. Fixation is part of the oral, anal and phallic phases, but not of life itself.

There is running and there is running away. The important thing is to be oneself in the present moment.

But that title...

"Again runner, then trail runner. Then again nothing. And again something. And again."

How to fall apart?

A reference to going flat out in a race and the pain of injury. To running into walls. Life as a succession of psychosocial crises and how to deal with them?

Not really, that's off topic.

"Life is joy. Sometimes it can be hard, but we must try to be happy. We must learn to endure the difficult moments. If you can, you can face everything. It requires lots of patience, but compared with this, trail running isn't much of a challenge," I remember Mira Rai saying.

EMBRACE THE SUCK, QUOI?

Curriculum vitae then.

Hmmm... No, too boring. I said just now that new sentences are constantly swishing through my head. Mainly snapshots of running kilometres from the past 33 years. And quotes from interviews, running books and clips I've read, listened to or watched over the years.

"I know that many long-distance runners carry stories in their backpacks."

I'm thinking. *Asphalt, mud, rocks & snow* gets to the heart of the matter, but sounds too flat (pun). Maybe something for the back flap?

Run (uphill)

No, too much like '*Run to the Hills*' by Iron Maiden, even though there's nothing wrong with 666. Every trail runner is a Beast.

I once asked a coach from my running club why he did his super long ultra-trails. How do you make the incomprehensible understandable? His answer was crystal clear. He didn't really like operating outside his comfort zone, but very often the world falls silent along the way. An existential purity that, like a snapshot, is an elusive star you unexpectedly land on. And certainly only when surrounded by nature, because asphalt is for cars.

Hmmm...

Asphalt is for cars is far from bad. Macho, but nicely so. Just like the unorthodox trail running manual *Never wipe your ass with a squirrel.*

Asphalt is for cars.

Perhaps...

No, too literary. Maybe as a quote for a promotion sticker?

THE HOLY TRAIL?

A suggestion from my publisher at our first meeting.

A nod to Monty Python. *The Holy Trail* is so in your face that it sticks. Let's google. Apparently it's the name of a 15 km trail race on the coastline of Holy Island in Wales. No other book as yet with that name. It may not be home-brewed, but vanity's no use here. Learn to compromise, Rik, especially with people with real expertise.

Yes!

The Holy Fucking Trail! The Fucking Holy Trail!

Hell, yeah!

Maybe in combination with a button *101 tips* on the flap? Commercially interesting, but won't it bury the character of my story? It's not a training manual at all? That's also not entirely true. It's bursting with beginners' mistakes and tips from a well-read enthusiast.

Compensate with a subtitle?

Running stories?
In a runner's shadow?
Inspiring running stories?

That sounds a bit arrogant. I sit back and sigh. What about *A rebel's running stories*?

No green light, because I don't want to collide with other running books.

Start to Burn!
Fail to Run!
Smile.

Quirky running stories? Hmmm, maybe that'll attract certain readers.

Am I actually still a trail runner?

My ultra in Chamonix is nine months ago. After that came a new position. Job coaching and interview training for young people. Again intensive people work, with far too long train commutes. With chocolate cakes, sandwiches and all kinds of fried food as comfort food on the way. Three stolen racing bikes and barely any running kilometres to my name. King Alcohol and Queen Music in my much too cosy bar. Starting to write this book. An idea for a new documentary, which after three promising meetings at a well-known production house died a silent death in their crowded agenda. In short: *The Never Ending Tour*, in the words of Bob Dylan's unending tour schedule since 1988.

What if I were to do something completely different? Even if only for a short period. Outdoor air and movement do me more good than computer work, I now know.

Professional dog walker?

Gardener?

I chase the job mart out of my head and return to the order of the day.

Established fact: I'm re-urbanized.

Maybe I should have stayed in Chamonix?

A good 10 kilos heavier. OK, 12 kilos to be honest. Possibly 15. Or more.

Welcome back, Mr Beer-Belly. Nice to meet you again. Everything OK? With Mrs Beer-Belly too, everything OK? And the kids too, all as it should be?

And greetings to Daddy Beer-Belly!

It all depends on how you look at it, but don't those extra kilos count as strength training for my rare runs? Ah, maybe I was just in too good physical shape – not an ounce of fat – for the OCC? Ironic, because I've never been so much involved with trail running as in recent months. Or at least in my head.

Decompression or shameless decay? *Et alors*?

I take a sip of coffee. The mug with the inscription 'The art is to live life as it comes' is a birthday present from my sister. I chuckle, remove my hands from the keyboard and reread my last paragraphs.

Maybe Big-Belly rather than Beer-Belly?

Did I know then that a year later I would get a similar mug with the inscription "To exist without wanting anything"?

My sister, the little bitch!

I rub my convex body.

CrossFit and chia seeds. Strava and Runkeeper. Boot camps and protein shakes. Fitbit around your arm and fitspiration on your Facebook wall. Too much movement and eating too healthily: is the pendulum about to swing back in our society? Right now it's as if *Gesundheit über alles* has become the new standard. I think back to my OCC. Everyone can go for a goal. Maybe I should look for a minimal effective dose?

"Do you ever stop running, Lizzy Hawker?"

"No, it's better to keep moving. Always moving. Life never stands still. It's a constant flow. It changes constantly. That's the challenge: learning to deal with it. Bending, without breaking."

"Is that the core of your life?"

"Exactly!" I hear the five-time UTMB® winner whispering in the back of my mind.

At work, as a job counsellor, I try in various ways to pierce through the *gangsta style* pose of my vulnerable teenagers. Especially by listening honestly and non-judgmentally. Sometimes with absurd humour, from time to time with a sledgehammer hit. Like when I dare to ask provocatively whether they want to stay boys or become men. Instinctive street language response, that guarantees the beginning of an authentic conversation. Social work may be a magnifying mirror of the way you function yourself. I don't think they realize how rhetorical this opening question is some days.

I'm actor, clown and psychologist. And - if it has to be - child. As someone said at an assessment meeting with my wards: "Rik sometimes plays more stupid than he is, but he does that to teach us something."

Caught in the act.

EVERYONE MESSES UP

Everyone messes up. And those who don't, know how to hide it well. Or sit tight.

Shit, this has become a typical thirties-something story.

Quitting smoking yet again.

Is my hairline still OK?

I know I function better if I move a little and spend less time at bars. As everyone knows. O beloved Belgium. O holy beer land of our fathers. How does François D'Haene of Team Salomon do it? He's both a specialist in long ultras and a winemaker!

"I don't want to ban the excessive, but to a culture that thinks that the only life that has value is the life that has been lived 200%, I say: 'Careful!' Life is like a pudding which has burned onto the cooking basin. Scrape it out too close to the basin and it will no longer taste good. Maybe we can taste the pudding without scraping?" says a media-minded psychiatrist in the radio interview once the thumping beat of Body Count has died away.

"It doesn't matter how fit or strong you are. The mountains will always find a way to humble you."

Maybe I need to return to the mountains this summer? Reconnect with silence and finish this manuscript. Which will justify a *Made in Chamonix-Mont-Blanc* button on the back flap.

Or stand as an alpinist on Mont Blanc instead of running around it again?
I click off the radio interview and open YouTube for The Verve.

No change, I can't change, I can't change, I can't change
But I'm here in my mould, I am here in my mould
But I'm a million different people from one day to the next
I can't change my mould, no, no, no, no, no, no, no.

"It doesn't matter how fit or strong you are. The mountains will always find a way to humble you. They offer you a different perspective. The immensity of the landscape confronts you with your own insignificance. As a human you are defenceless here. If you are open to it, the mountains will place you with your feet nicely on the ground. They always have something to teach you, believe me," Lizzy Hawker says.

Could it be that mountains consist not of rock, snow and ice, but of pieces of ourselves?

I re-read the chapters I've written so far. My new running shoes have been waiting for two weeks in a corner of my apartment. I close my laptop and pull them on.

FUCK IT

Done with feeling smaller or bigger than I am.

An old crocodile that bites its own tail still has sharp teeth.

Half an hour to start again.

And let's stick with *The Holy Trail.* ▲▲▲

WORD OF THANKS

Writing a book is a solitary process, but getting it into print is not something you do on your own. Without the contributions and input of a whole number of people, this book would never have seen the light of day. Let me expressly thank a number of them here.

Lannoo Publishers took me on board after I presented them with some initial columns of The Holy Trail . Together with publisher Johan Ghysels, I developed the format and structure, with a bucket list of headings to flesh out with interviews and narrative. The trust with which he sent me back to my writing table was a great stimulus. During the writing process, I got support from editor Yaele Vanhuyse, who could always be counted on to think things through with me, and who helped me keep an overall perspective on the project and respect the timing. The layout is by Wim De Dobbeleer, the English translation by Michael Lomax.

The Ghent outdoor sports store Avventura, along with Elements, its partner in sustainable and ecological outdoor material, advised and supported me in the logistics field.

A big thank you also to the twelve trail runners who were ready to share their competition experience with me. I will remember for a long time to come the interviews in people's homes, in cafés or via Skype, and the many knowing chuckles in my interviewees' eyes.

I end this books with a final word of thanks to all family, friends, physiotherapists, osteopaths, psychologists and café owners who patched me up when something got broken. ▲▲▲

BIBLIOGRAPHY

AUDIOVISUAL MEDIA

Arc'teryx, 'MOVE' (a Duct Tape Then Beer production), in *www.youtube.com*, 30 September 2013.

Arc'teryx, 'Silence' (a Duct Tape Then Beer production), in *www.youtube.com*, 18 March 2013.

Arc'teryx, 'The Lion & The Gazelle' (a Duct Tape Then Beer production), in *www.youtube.com*, 7 July 2014.

Billy Yang Films, '15 Hours | with Anton Krupicka', in *www.youtube.com*, 21 May 2015.

Fjord Norway, 'Killian Jornet in his new Norwegian backyard' in *www.youtube.com*, 20 December 2016.

Giler, N., 'Mustang trail race', in *www.vimeo.com*, 2014.

Grillon, D., 'TRAIL - UTMB® - OCC - Inside the Race – Gopro', in *www.youtube.com*, 10 October 2016.

Guillaume Arthus, 'Beer Ultra 2016', in *www.youtube.com*, 5 July 2016.

Hargreaves, B., 'Cliff Young' in *www.youtube.com*, 6 February 2009.

Icicle, 'Kilian Jornet 4hr 57min Mont Blanc record', in *www.youtube.com*, 11 July 2013.

Jean Michel Faure Vincent, 'Marathon du Mont Blanc 2014 (a Mousse Production)', in *www.youtube.com*, 1 July 2014.

Kilianjornet, *Instagram*.

Marathon du Mont-Blanc, '40km – Résumé global en images – Marathon du Mont-Blanc 2014', in *www.youtube.com*, 1 July 2014.

Marathon du Mont-Blanc, 'KM Vertical 2017 – 1000m de sensations!', in *www.youtube.com*, 27 October 2017.

Mercedes-Benz, 'Kilian Jornet: up in the mountains with the Marco Polo - Mercedes-Benz original', in *www.youtube.com*, 16 December 2015.

Relaas, 'Martin Vereecken steekt ze allemaal voorbij', in *www.relaas.be*, 12 November 2015.

Run Steep Get High, 'The 2016 0CC – Osiers – Champex – Chamonix', in *www.youtube.com*, 30 August 2016.

Runners' High, 'UTMB® / OCC 2014 interview - RUNNERS HIGH', in *www.youtube.com*, 29 August 2014.

Salomon Spain, 'Video Oficial Zegama 2017', in *www.youtube.com*, 13 June 2017.

Salomon TrailRunning, 'Zegama 2013 English subtitles, in *www.youtube.com*, 26 June 2013.

Salomon TV, 'SalomonTV: Dream Trip: Nepal', in *www.youtube.com*, 23 May 2017.

Salomon TV, 'Zegama-Aizkorri 2014, official video', in *www.youtube.com*, 6 June 2014.

SalomonTrailRunning, 'Fast and Light - Salomon Running TV S04 E08', in *www.youtube.com*, 20 October 2015.

SalomonTrailRunning, 'Kilian's Quest S3 E06 - How I prepare an Ultra', in *www.youtube.com*, 15 August 2011.

SalomonTrailRunning, 'Why We Run - Salomon Running TV S3 E01', in *www.youtube.com*, 30 October 2013.

Suunto, 'Kilian Jornet - How do I train (again and again)', in *www.youtube.com*, 9 January 2018.

TED, 'Are we born to run? | Christopher McDougall', in *www.youtube.com*, 4 February 2011.

TEDx Talks, 'The runner's low - depression & the badwater ultra marathon: Hannah Roberts at TEDxHonolulu, in *www.youtube.com*, 25 January 2014.

The Fruitarian, 'Ultra Running lecture by Michael Arnstein PART 1, in *www.youtube.com*, 11 October 2011.

The North Face®, 'Curiosity', in *www.youtube.com*, 25 Semptember 2015.

The North Face®, 'The North Face®: The Power In Me – Always Moving', in *www.youtube.com*, 1 April 2015.

Tomtesterom, 'Marathon des Sables (S02E06)', in *www.youtube.com*, 7 August 2013.

Tor des Géants®, 'Tor des Géants® – Official Video Report', in *www.youtube.com*, 2 October 2017.

Ultra-Trail du Mont-Blanc®, 'OCC 2015 – Race report', in *www.youtube.com*, 28 August 2015.

Ultra-Trail du Mont-Blanc®, 'UTMB® Stars - Dawa Sherpa story on UTMB®', in *www.youtube.com*, 4 May 2017.

Videos4Motivation, 'Cliff Young Shuffle - Ultramarathon Runner - Never Give Up!' in *www.youtube.com*, 29 June 2012.

Wildplans, 'Darkness: how ultrarunning can strip away our emotional barriers', in *www.youtube.com*, 16 June 2013.

BOOKS

Albers, I., *De god van het lopen*, Atlas Contact, Amsterdam, 2013.

Cuppen, H., *Liefdesbang - Overwin verlatingsangst en bindingsangst*, Uitgeverij Ankhermes, Utrecht, 2014.

De Wachter, D., *De Wereld van De Wachter*, Lannoo Campus, Leuven, 2016.

De Wachter, D., *Liefde. Een onmogelijk verlangen*, Lannoo Campus, Leuven 2014.

Doumen, S. and Smeester, H., *Start to Run met Evy Gruyaert – Fit en gezond in 10 weken*, Lannoo, Tielt, 2011.

Geurtz, G., *Verslaafd aan liefde – de weg naar zelfacceptatie en geluk in relaties*, Ambo-Anthos, Amsterdam, 2009.

Gryson, M. and De Waele, V., *Positief agressief – Hoe woede benutten*, Lannoo Campus, Leuven, 2017.

Hawker, L., *Runner – A short story about a long run*, Aurum Press, London, 2015.

Jones, K., *Trail Running Chamonix and the Mont Blanc region – 40 routes in the Chamonix Valley, Italy and Switzerland*, Cicerone, Milnthorpe, 2016.

Jornet, K., *Run or Die*, Velopress, Boulder, 2013.

Jurek, S. and Friedman, S., *Eat & Run: my unlikely journey to ultramarathon greatness*, Bloomsbury Publishing PLC, New York, 2013.

Karnazes, D., *Ultramarathon Man: Confessions of an All-Night Runner*, Tarcher/Penguin, New York, 2006.

Les Sentiers de Grande Randonnée asbl, *Topo-Guide du sentier de Grande Randonnée – Vallée de l'Ourthe et Sentier du Nord (GR57)*, European Graphics SA, La Louvière, 2008.

Mayhew, B. and Bindloss, J. , *Trekking in the Nepal Himalaya – 30 great treks*, Lonely Planet Publications Pty Ltd, 2009.

McDougall, C., Born to Run: *A Hidden Tribe, Superathletes, and the Greatest Race the World Has Never Seen*, Knopf, New York, 2009.

Murakami, H., *Waarover ik praat als ik over hardlopen praat*, Atlas Contact, Amsterdam, 2015.

Robillard, J., *Never Wipe Your Ass with a Squirrel: A Trail Running, Ultramarathon, and Wilderness Survival Guide for Weird Folks*, Createspace Independent Publishing Platform, 2013.

FILMS

In the High Country (2013, director: Joel Wolpert).

Mira (2016, director: Lloyd Belcher).

Summits Of My Life I: A Fine Line (2012, director: Sébastien Montaz-Rosset).

Summits Of My Life II: Déjame Vivir (2014, director: Sébastien Montaz-Rosset).

Summits Of My Life III: Langtang (2015, director: Sébastien Montaz-Rosset).

The Barkley Marathons: The Race That Eats Its Young (2014, director: Annika Iltis and Timothy James Kane).

The Unknown – The Hardrock 100 (2017, director: Billie Yang).

The Why – Running 100 Miles (2018, director: Billie Yang).

INTERVIEWS*

Anna Edward, Pollença – Spain.

Bart De Weirdt, Ghent – Belgium.

Brian Lang, New York – United States.

Darianne Spittaels & Lotte Spittaels, Ghent
– Belgium.

Eduard Serrano, Barcelona – Spain.

Erica Rusbridge, Perth – Australia.

Jennifer Gale, Ormeau – Australia.

Kris Van De Velde, Bejing – China.

Marc Weening, Doorwerth – Netherlands.

Mario Ramos, Lima – Peru.

Martin Vereecken, Gentbrugge – Belgium.

Michiel Panhuysen, The Hague – Netherlands.

*All interviews for The Holy Trail were conducted
between September and December 2017. Author
Rik Merchie interviewed the Belgian trail-runners in person. He called the foreign trail-runners
by phone and/or via Skype.

ONLINE

Van Lieshout, A., 'Trailrun tips voor beginners', in
www.prorun.nl, 7 August 2016.

s.n., '7 trailrunning tips voor beginners', in
www.glowmagazine.nl, 12 April 2016.

Ooninckx, J., 'Trailrunning, iets voor jou? Info
beginners', in *www.trail-running.eu*, s.d.

Hadfield, J., '21 Quick Trail Running Tips', in
www.runnersworld.com, 23 May 2014.

Hay, D., '6 Things Every Beginner Should Know
Before Trail Running', in *www.rockcreekrunner.com*,
2 November 2012.

Van De Velde, D., '5 tips voor beginnnende trail-
runners', in *www.sport.be*, 28 March 2017.

Krupicka, A. and Scholes, F., '10 Tips for Running
Your First Ultramarathon', in *www.redbull.com*,
29 September 2017.

Corless, I., 'Tromso SkyRace 2016 Summary
and Images – Skyrunner Extreme Series', in
www.iancorless.org, 6 August 2016.

Proston, A., 'Just Another Goat: Sedona,
Brazil and El Cruce Columbia 2014', in
www.amysproston.blogspot.be, 11 April 2014.

s.n., 'Race director clarifies final outcome of 2017
Barkley Marathons', in *www.runningmagazine.ca*,
4 April 2017.

s.n., 'Leadville Trail 100 History', in
www.endthetrendnow.com, s.d.

Mig, 'Barkley race report: Where dreams come to
die', in *www.mudsweatrails.nl*, 7 April 2016.

Mig, 'Column 100% Mig', in *www.mudsweatrails.nl*,
8 January 2016.

Mig, 'Stranger than Paradise – PTL 2017', in
www.mudsweatrails.nl, 5 September 2017.

Mig, 'Barkley Marathons (USA)', in
www.mudsweatrails.nl, 11 April 2011.

s.n., 'Marathon du Mont-Blanc : Kilian Jornet
victorieux, in *www.marathons.fr*, 2 July 2012.

Van Der Meulen, K., 'Emelie Forsberg: 3 trailrunning tips van 's werelds beste', in *www.mindlift.com*,
5 July 2014.

Turley, B., 'Race Report: Cappadocia Ultra Trail',
in *www.eashle.wordpress.com*, 15 November 2016.

Hutchinson, C., 'Do Drinkers Exercise More Than
Their Sober Peers?', in *www.abcnews.go.com*,
31 August 2009.

Schneekloth, M., 'Race Report – 2017 Everest Trail
Race® (Stage 1)', in *www.ultrakrautrunning.com*,
11 September 2017.

Mahoney, E., 'UTMB® 2016 Results: Another successful & action-packed year for the UTMB®', in
www.chamonet.com, 29 August 2016.

Smith, S, 'Tarawera 100K Race Report: A
Trip That Was a Journey and a Stumble', in
www.therunnerstrip.com, 14 February 2015.

Dan, '2013 Vibram Hong Kong 100 Race Report
– The rise of ultra-marathons in Asia', in
www.ultra168.com, 22 January 2013.

s.n., 'GR 57 Ourthe Noordpad: voorstelling', in
www.trekkings.be, s.d.

McIntosh, F., 'Cape Town Ultra-Trail Run', in
www.nightjartravel.com, October 2014.

Corless, I., 'Cycling for Runners – The
Introduction', in *www.iancorless.org*,
19 September 2014.

Languin, I., '1966: un Boeing d'Air India s'écrase
sur les flancs du Mont-Blanc', in *www.tdg.ch*,
23 January 2016.

Hawker, L., 'A Spiritual Journey', in
www.runnersworld.co.uk, November 2013.

Watt, J., 'Region: Nepal, Mustang, Konchog
Ling Cave Paintings', in *www.himalayanart.org*,
May 2013.

Beinhorn, G., 'Born to Booze – Are the
Tarahumara Worthy Role Models?', in
www.joyfulathlete.com, 2 March 2011.

Jhung, L., 'The Many Layers Of Ultrarunning Star Anton Krupicka', in *www.running.competitor.com*, 19 June 2017.

Corless, I., 'Kilian Jornet to race in the UK at Salomon Glen Coe Skyline', in *www.iancorless.org*, 22 March 2017.

Reymen, N., 'Willen of niet, we worden zwijnen tijdens de après-ski. Waarom toch?', in *www.demorgen.be*, 12 October 2017.

Chaes, A., 'On the Trail... At Trail des Templiers – Consuming stinky cheese on the trails', in *www.runnersworld.com*, 1 March 2006.

Carraz, M., '80km du Mont Blanc race recap', in *www.ultrarunningcommunity.com*, s.d.

Lung, J., 'Golden Hour Dreams (or Nightmares): The 2017 Western States 100-Mile Endurance Run Race Report', in *www.therunfactory.com*, s.d.

Butter, N., 'Marathon des Sables Race Report', in *www.nickbutterrunning.com*, 20 April 2016.

Scholtz, R., 'Otter African Trail Run: Retto Challlenge 2016 race report' in *www.touchandgo.com*, 2 December 2016.

SONG LYRICS

Blur (1997) *Song 2*. Food Records.

Deftones (1997) *My Own Summer (Shove It)*. Maverick.

Foo Fighters (1999) *Learn to Fly*. Roswell/RCA.

Foo Fighters (2017) *Run*. RCA.

Gorky (1992) *Ria*. Parlophone Music Belgium.

Millionaire (2005) *I'm On A High*. PIAS.

Moby (1999) *Run On*. Mute Records & V2 Records.

Queens of the Stone Age (2000) *Feel Good Hit of the Summer*. Interscope Records.

Radiohead (2000) *Idioteque*. Parlophone.

Red Hot Chili Peppers (1999) *Californication*. Warner Music.

Samantha Fu (2001) *Theme From Discotheque*. PIAS.

Sepultura (1996) *Roots Bloody Roots*. Roadrunner Records.

Spinvis (2002) *Astronaut*. Excelsior Recordings.

Steak Number Eight (2011) *Pyromaniac*. Keremos.

The Avalanches (2000) *Frontier Psychiatrist*. Modular Recordings.

The Streets (2006) *Never Went to Church*. 679 Artists.

The Verve (1997) *Bitter Sweet Symphony*. Hut Records.

Therapy? (1998) *Straight Life*. A&M Records.

U2 (1987) *Where the Streets Have No Name*. Islands Records.

Underworld (1995) *Born Slippy*. Junior Boy's Own.

Zing Mee Met JB (2014) *Kapot*. Botrange Records.

WEBSITES

www.beermile.com
www.betrail.run
www.cappadociaultratrail.com
www.chamonix.com
www.elcrucecolumbia.com
www.emelieforsberg.com
www.everesttrailrace.com
www.festivaldestempliers.com
www.hardrock100.com
www.hk100-ultra.com
www.i-tra.org
www.kilianjornet.cat
www.leadvilleraceseries.com
www.marathondessables.com
www.matterhorn.ultraks.ch
www.montblancmarathon.net
www.mudsweattrails.nl
www.mustangtrailrace.com
www.normal-runner.com

www.otter.run
www.randos-montblanc.com
www.skylinescotland.com
www.skyrunnerworldseries.com
www.skyrunning.com
www.summitsofmylife.com
www.tarawtraultra.co.nz
www.tordesgeants.it
www.trailattitudefamennoise.be
www.trailrunningnepal.org
www.tromsoskyrace.com
www.ultratourmonterosa.com
www.ultratrail-worldtour.com
www.ultratrail.it
www.ultratrailkathmandu.com
www.utmbmontblanc.com
www.wser.org
www.zegama-aizkorri.com

PHOTO CREDITS*

Ana Edward   p 56

Anuj Dhoj Adhikery 2016 (via Ultra Tour Monte Rosa)   p 6-7

Brian Lang   p 22

Craig Kolesky (via Ultra-Trail Cape Town®)   p 140-141, 147 (above)

Daniel Petty (Denver Post)   p 10-11

Diego Winitzky (via Zegama Aizkorri)   p 80-81, 84-85

Eduard Serrano   p 82

El Cruce Columbia   p 28-29, 30, 32-33, 35, 38-39

Erica Rusbridge   p 166

Geoffrey Meuli   p 128-129, 132-133, 134-135

Giacomo Buzio (via Tor des Géants®)   p 173

Glenn Tachiyama   p 90-91

Greg Alric (via Festival des Templiers)   p 108-109, 174-175

Grégory Yetchmeniza (Photopqr/MaxPPP)   p 154-155, 189

Guillem Casanova Bosch   p 40-41, 52-53, 68-69, 72-73, 118-119, 152-153 and ends

Jacques Marais (via Otter Trail)   p 190-191

Javi Bodas (via Tromsø Skyrace)   p 20-21

Jean-Philippe Ksiazek (AFP/Belga)   p 182

Jean-Pierre Clatot (AFP/Belga)   p 62-63

Jeff Pachoud (AFP/Belga)   p 158-159

Jennifer Gale   p 112

Jonathan Koutstaal   p 46

Jordi Villa (via Everest Trail Race®)   p 120-121

Kris Van De Velde   p 130

Maindru Photo   p 188

Marc Weening   p 70, 76

Mario Ramos   p 156

Martin Vereecken   p 100

Matt Trappe (via Tarawera Ultra Marathon)   p 110-111, 114-115

Mustang Mountain Trial Race   p 164-165, 166, 168-169

Pierre Lucianaz (Tor des Géants®)   p 66-67

Rik Merchie   p 13, 27, 88, 96-97, 123, 124, 127, 139, 151, 161, 171, 172, 177

Salomon Cappadocia Ultra-Trail®   p 98-99, 102-103, 104-105

Sebastien Chaigneau (via Lavaredo Ultra Trail)   p 54-55

Stefano Jeantet (via Tor des Géants®)   p 16-17

The Washington Post   p 44-45, 48-49

Trail de la Grimace   p 78

Ultra-trail Cape Town®   p 142

Xavier Briel (via Ultra-Trail Cape Town®)   p 144-145, 146, 147 (below)

Every effort has been made to trace the copyright holders of material quoted and reproduced in this book.
    If application is made in writing to the publisher, any omissions will be included in future edtions..

WWW.ULTRATOURMONTEROSA.COM

WWW.HARDROCK100.COM

WWW.TORDESGEANTS.IT

WWW.TROMSOSKYRACE.COM

WWW.ELCRUCECOLUMBIA.COM

WWW.SKYLINESCOTLAND.COM

WWW.BARKLEYMARATHONS.COM

WWW.ULTRATRAIL.IT

WWW.MONTBLANCMARATHON.NET

WWW.LEADVILLERACESERIES.COM

WWW.ZEGAMA-AIZKORRI.COM

WWW.WSER.ORG

WWW.CAPPADOCIAULTRATRAIL.COM

WWW.TARAWERAULTRA.CO.NZ

WWW.EVERESTTRAILRACE.COM

WWW.HK100-ULTRA.COM

WWW.ULTRATRAILCAPETOWN.COM

WWW.MATTERHORN.ULTRAKS.CH

WWW.UTMBMONTBLANC.COM

WWW.MUSTANGTRAILRACE.COM

WWW.FESTIVALDESTEMPLIERS.COM

WWW.MARATHONDESSABLES.COM

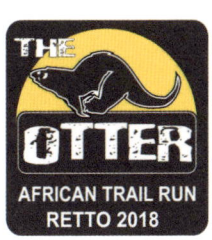

WWW.OTTER.RUN

www.lannoo.com

Register on our website and we will send you a regular newsletter
with information about new books and interesting, exclusive offers.

If you have comments or questions, please contact our editorial team at:
redactielifestyle@lannoo.com

© Uitgeverij Lannoo nv, Tielt, 2018 and Rik Merchie

Layout   *English translation*
Wim De Dobbeleer   Michael Lomax

D/2018/45/534 – NUR 480
ISBN 978 94 014 4920 5

CONVERSION TABLES

KILOMETRES	MILES
5KM	3MI 188.07YD
10KM	6MI 376.13YD
15KM	9MI 564.20YD
20KM	12MI 752.27YD
25KM	15MI 940.33YD
30KM	18MI 1128.4YD
35KM	21MI 1316.5YD
40KM	24MI 1504.5YD
45KM	27MI 1692.6YD
50KM	31MI 120.66YD
55KM	34MI 308.73YD
60KM	37MI 496.80YD
65KM	40MI 684.86YD
70KM	43MI 872.93YD
75KM	46MI 1061.0YD
80KM	49MI 1249.1YD
85KM	52MI 1437.1YD
90KM	54MI 1625.2YD
95KM	59MI 53.26YD
100KM	62MI 241.33YD

METRES	FOOT
1,000M	3,280.84FT
2,000M	6,561.68FT
3,000M	9,842.52FT
4,000M	13,123.36FT
5,000M	16,404.20FT
6,000M	19,685.04FT
7,000M	22,965.88FT
8,000M	26,246.72FT
9,000M	29,527.56FT
10,000M	32,808.40FT
11,000M	36,089.24FT
12,000M	39,370.08FT
13,000M	42,650.92FT
14,000M	45,931.76FT
15,000M	49,212.60FT
16,000M	52,493.44FT
17,000M	55,774.28FT
18,000M	59,055.12FT
19,000M	62,335.96FT
20,000M	65,616.80FT